The Way It Was
The North Dakota Frontier Experience
Book Four: Germans from Russia Settlers

Published in the Series

The Way It Was:
The North Dakota Frontier Experience

Book One: The Sod-busters, 1996

Book Two: Norwegian Homesteaders, 1998

Book Three: The Cowboys & Ranchers, 1999

Book Four: Germans From Russia Settlers, 1999

Book Five: Native People, 2002

Coming in 2003

Book Six: The Townspeople

The Way It Was

The North Dakota Frontier Experience
Book Four:
Germans from Russia Settlers

Everett C. Albers and D. Jerome Tweton, Editors

THE GRASS ROOTS PRESS
Fessenden, North Dakota 58438
Second Printing, 2002

This book is dedicated to Rose Marie Fiechtner Henke, a *Volksdeutsche* who married a *Reichsdeutscher*, Warren A. Henke. *"Vielen Dank,"* Henkes, *"Danke sehr!"* The series is dedicated to the memory of North Dakota pioneers.

Editors: *Everett C. Albers and D. Jerome Tweton*
Designer: *Otto Design of Bismarck, ND*
Printer: *Hignell Book Printing of Winnipeg, Manitoba, Canada*

Published by The Grass Roots Press

Printed in Canada

10 9 8 7 6 5 4 3 2

International Standard Book Number: 0-9650778-4-5 (Book 4)
International Standard Book Number: 0-9650778-1-0 (6-Volume Set)

Library of Congress Catalog Card Number: 99-091525

Acknowledgments

*T*HE EDITORS THANK Timothy Kloberdanz for his insightful writing on the Germans from Russia and for his willingness to answer questions. We thank Michael Miller of The Germans from Russia Heritage Collection of North Dakota State University Libraries for his assistance in finding appropriate photographs, including the color rendition of the drawings from the July 11, 1896, *Harper's Weekly* featured on the cover. Rachael Schmidt of the Germans from Russia Heritage Society in Bismarck graciously loaned us materials from the Society's excellent library. We thank the reference librarians at the State Historical Society of North Dakota for their continued assistance as we come back again and again to the WPA collection of interviews. We acknowledge the sources of photographs and maps in this volume throughout — including those remarkable local historical societies who have done so much to document Dakota culture. We especially thank the American Historical Society of Germans from Russia for permission to reprint the photographs found in Dr. Karl Stumpp's *The German-Russians*. Once again, we thank the Institute for Regional Studies at North Dakota State University and its archivist John E. Bye who placed the magnificent Fred Hultstrand History in Pictures Collection in the American Memory Collection of the Library of Congress on the Internet for the world to appreciate.

About the editing . . .

We editors have made every effort to select a representative sample of the German-Russian settlers' experience from the 5,000 interviews collected in the late 1930s. We have recast those rewritten in third-person back to first-person and changed a few sentences, but the words remain those of the pioneers. Any errors are ours, not theirs.

Table of Contents

In Search of a Better Life: The Germans From Russia   *D. Jerome Tweton*   *i-ix*

"Arbeit Macht Das Leben Süss — "   *Everett C. Albers*   *x-xii*

Finding an International Language   *The Franz Baumgartners*   *1-2*

Fighting the Worst of Prairie Fires   *The Johannas Baumgartners*   *3-6*

Stealing the County Seat: Emmons County Battle   *Jacob Fisher (by son Mathias)*   *7-10*

Hardship and Heartache on the Homestead   *The August Flegel Family*   *11-18*

When a *Volksdeutsche* Marries a *Reichsdeutcher*   *Minnie Sperling Freitag*   *19-22*

Searching for Good Land in Logan County   *Johann Gutschmidt*   *23-26*

Homesteading, Pre-empting, and Tree
Claiming in Dickey County   *Simon Hille*   *27-32*

From Bessarabia to Northern Dakota:
A Family's Journey   *The Gottlieb Isaak Family*   *33-40*

Looking for Water: From Hague Settlement
to Buffalo Lake   *Max Keller*   *41-47*

Teaching in Russia, Farming in McHenry County:
The Saga of a *Wohyniendeutsche* Couple   *Adolf Klebe*   *48-51*

Working the Land and Working for God   *The Gottfried Kurtz Family*   *52-56*

Farming with Oxen — Photographs   *Fred Hultstrand History in Pictures Collection*   *57*

The *Dobrudschadeutsche* from Russia   *The George & August Leitner Families*   *58-63*

Not All Homestead Life was Drab and Humorless   *The Christian Maiers*   *64-68*

A Colony in Search of a Better Life   *The Johann Millers*   *69-73*

Finding Prosperity on a Plains Homestead   *Philip and Eva Mosbrucker*   *74-78*

The Mennonite Experience in Cavalier County   *The Spenst Family*   *79-84*

From Selz to Selz and Trouble with Creditors   *Balzar Thomas*   *85-87*

A Second Boom Homesteader   *Morris Weisgarber*   *88-90*

Index and About the editors . . .   *91-93*

D. Jerome Tweton

In Search of a Better Life: The Germans From Russia

D. Jerome Tweton

"Der Erste hat den Tod,
Der Zweite hat die Not,
Der Dritte erst hat Brot."

"For the first generation, there is death.
For the second, there is want.
Only for the third is there bread."

DURING THE YEARS THAT I TAUGHT North Dakota history at the University of North Dakota, one of the topics that baffled students was the Germans from Russia. What in the world were Germans doing in Russia? Why would they want to leave the fertile lands north of the Black Sea? Why did they come in such great numbers to North Dakota?

The story of the Germans from Russia is one of the most interesting chapters in our state's history. First of all, why were there thousands upon thousands of Germans in Russia? Catherine the Great, Russian ruler from 1762 to 1796, wanted very much to populate the

Catherine The Great

i

lower Volga River and Black Sea region of southern Russia with people who would strengthen her empire's agricultural economy and serve as a buffer against the Turks. Since she herself was of German royal ancestry, she especially looked to the German states for would-be settlers.

In 1763 she issued a manifesto that within a short time lured over 30,000 Germans to the fertile lands of southern and Volga Russia. She offered free land, exemption from service in the Russian army, religious freedom, local self-government, and tax exemptions. In other words, Germans in Russia could remain German and not become Russian. With this inducement, Russian recruiters met with great success in the German states. Germans continued to migrate to Russia in significant numbers until the reign of Tsar Alexander II who ruled the empire from 1855 to 1881.

Why, having settled in Russia and having achieved success after decades, even generations, of hardship, did so many Germans leave Russia? Tsar Alexander II decided that the Russian Empire needed modernization. Toward that goal he abruptly curtailed the special privileges

German Women On a Lunch Break in the Harvest Field in Russia
From Dr. Karl Stumpp, **The German-Russians**, *translated by Joseph S. Height*
(Lincoln, Nebraska: Reprint by the
American Historical Society of Germans from Russia, 1978).

D. Jerome Tweton

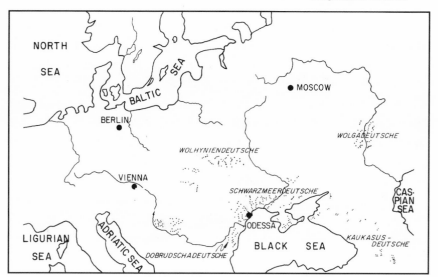

The Volksdeutsche *in Poland and Russia*
From **Plains Folk: North Dakota's Ethnic History**
(Fargo, North Dakota: North Dakota Institute for Regional Studies, 1988).

TSAR Alexander II

that the Germans had enjoyed for a century. In 1864 he introduced the *zemstvo* system which ended German self-government. Ten years later in 1874 German exemption from the Russian army came to an end. Tsar Alexander III, who came to the throne in 1881, expanded efforts to modernize the empire. His main objective was the assimilation of minority groups into mainstream society. In 1892 all schools, government *and* parochial, came under the control of the state and Russian became the language of instruction. Put simply, the Germans were to be Russified.

As obnoxious and intolerable as these actions by the Tsar were, land shortage and economic distress played the key roles in the out-migration of German-Russian people. Farms were small, and as time passed, it became obvious that fourth and fifth generation Germans could not support themselves on the "family farm." Many were and many would become landless. Some moved inland, as far as Siberia, in the search for new farm lands. Others looked across the ocean for the solution to their problem. To be sure, the political situation was a powerful reason for emigration, as witnessed in several of the recollec-

iii

tions in this book, but the possibility of good, free land was even more powerful.

Why, then, did these Germans come in such great numbers to North Dakota? In 1872 Johann Bette, who had immigrated from the Black Sea region to America in 1849, returned to southern Russia and spread the word about the availability of homestead land in the United States. That same year several families immigrated, staying with Bette in Ohio that first winter. The group sent out a land-scouting party which returned with the report that the best unsettled land was in Dakota Territory. These Black Sea Germans took up land northwest of Yankton in the neighborhood of Scotland. By 1884 the ensuing flood of Black Sea immigrants pushed their homesteading frontier into present-day North Dakota. Almost all came to live in what has been called the German-Russian Triangle (see map below — essay continues on page vi).

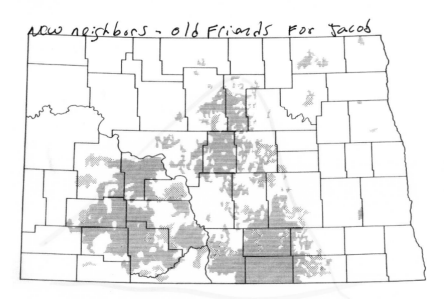

The German-Russian Triangle — Settlement in North Dakota
Shaded area indicates where the Germans from Russia settled in the state.
The 1895 map on the facing page includes county and town names
found in the stories of the settlers included in this book
(some counties were renamed or divided, many of the towns no longer exist).
From William C. Sherman, **Prairie Mosaic**
(Fargo, North Dakota: North Dakota Institute for Regional Studies, 1983).

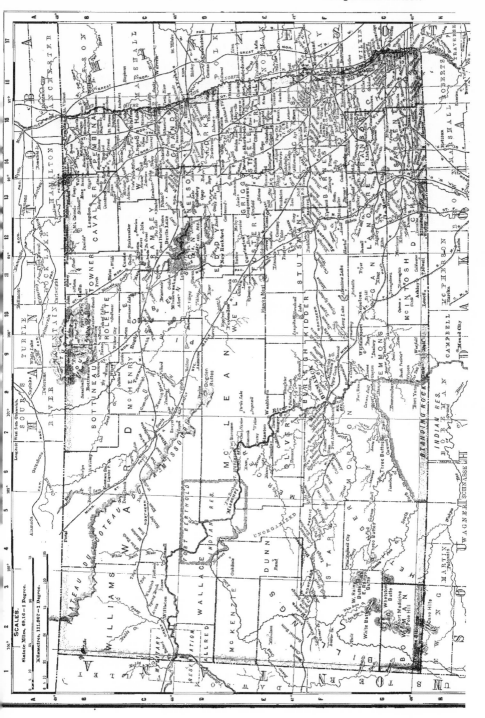

In his perceptive chapter, "Volksdeutche, the Eastern European Germans," in *Plains Folk, North Dakota's Ethnic History* (1988), Timothy J. Kloberdanz points out ten characteristics of the Black Sea German settlement of the Northern Great Plains.

One: Scouts spied out the land to make sure that suitable homesteads could be claimed. No other ethnic group that settled North Dakota used scouts as extensively as did the Black Sea Germans.

Two: They avoided living in cities; they came to farm! This was not as true for other immigrant groups such as the Norwegians or Swedes or *Reichsdeutsche.* True, most of these people did farm, but some chose to live in towns such as Fargo or Grand Forks which developed small ethnic neighborhoods.

Three: The Black Sea Germans had an appreciation of treeless, level landscapes, preferring the wide-open plains. Scandinavians and Germans, on the other hand, had to adjust psychologically to that landscape, choosing when possible the wooded banks of rivers and a topography that was not flat.

Four: The Germans from the Black Sea "desired to have a closed colony type of settlement." Much more than the other immigrant groups, these people sought out land that allowed them to establish tightly-knit communities. Of course, all the immigrants tended to settle near to others from their respective homelands: Poles near Poles, Icelanders near Icelanders, etc. This was natural and comfortable.

Five: They established homesteads alongside fellow Germans of similar religious beliefs. Unlike the Scandinavians, who were almost all Lutheran, the Germans were a diverse religious people: Roman Catholic, Lutheran, Mennonite, Baptist. Since their settlements in Russia were organized along religious lines, they continued that division in the New World.

Six: "Regional ties were especially pronounced among Black Sea Germans." They tended to settle in ways that reflected their village or regional background in Russia. Old World village affiliation meant much less to Scandinavians, Poles, or Germans, largely because their homeland social structure was not as close as that of the Black Sea Germans.

Seven: They "might rightly be called cultural chauvinists." "Social cohesion" was of the highest value. Black Sea Germans who were interviewed by the WPA in the 1930s all married within their religious faith and only one married a non-German from Russia — that person married a Reich German.

Eight: "The Black Sea emigration was primarily a movement of families." As the interviews in this book demonstrate, the colony or several-family approach to settlement was quite common. Rare was the single family or person who made the journey to America alone. In contrast, this was not common among the Scandinavian groups, the Germans, or the Poles.

Nine: They were "a people on the move." They were not afraid to pull up stakes and journey to what they considered to be a better place. For a people who went from Germany to Russia to America, migrating from southern North Dakota to northern North Dakota or to Canada was just a short hop. Other immigrant groups tended to stay put once they had taken up land.

Ten: The Black Sea migration pattern was from south to north. Almost all these Germans entered North Dakota through South Dakota; even within the state the pattern remained south to north. This was contrary to the usual east to west movement of the other immigrant groups.

These characteristics that Professor Kloberdanz presents were generally true for the non-Black Sea Germans as well. There were, however, exceptions. The Germans from the Caucasus region often emigrated as single families. The Dobrudja Black Sea Germans (the western shore of the Sea on lands held by Turkey) first came to North Dakota through Canada. The same was true of some German-Russian Mennonites.

By 1920 nearly 70,000, about 25 percent of all those who came to America, Germans from Russia had found homes in North Dakota. The lion's share, perhaps as high as 95 percent, hailed from southern Russia — the Black Sea region. There were, however, other groups of

Germans from Russia who immigrated to the United States and carved out farms in North Dakota.

Germans who settled around Mariupol on the Sea of Azon, just northeast of the Crimea, faced a land-shortage crisis in the 1890s, and many left for the United States. Never great in numbers, most settled in Stutsman County around Courtenay.

The Dobrudja Germans were a landless group who left the Odessa area in southern Russia for the Turkish region of Dobrudja on the western shores of the Black Sea. Under Turkish rule they enjoyed relatively good times. After the Russo-Turkish War in 1877, the region became part of Rumania and the good times came to an end. The Rumanians, unlike the Turks, proved to be unpleasant, restrictive rulers. In the early 1880s the Dobrudja Germans began to immigrate to the New World. They came to North Dakota through Canada to Foster County and then to their permanent homesteads in Wells County.

Argue with Sonya's Family [handwritten annotation]

German-Russian Mennonites especially were disturbed by the new policy of mandatory military service which was patently contrary to their religious thinking. Their migration began in the early 1870s and reached high tide around 1880. Large Mennonite colonies had been established in southern Manitoba in the late 1870s and early 1880s. In 1888 a few began to homestead in the Cavalier County townships of Moscow, Gordon, and Henderson.

The Volga Germans, the Caucasus Germans, and the Volhynian Germans never came in great numbers to North Dakota. The Volga Germans were the first immigrants to leave Germany for Russia in the 1760s. Land shortage and crop failures induced many of them to leave the Lower Volga for America. Most settled in Kansas and Nebraska, but a few came to North Dakota between 1900 and 1914. They found land in several locations: around Carson, Denhoff, Englevale, and in Cavalier County. The Caucasus Germans usually migrated one family at a time between 1900 and 1914. Those few who came to North Dakota settled in the south central counties and around Anamoose. Volhynian Germans who resided in Polish Russia came to North Dakota between 1890 and 1914. Few in numbers, they obtained scattered land claims mostly in Cavalier and Pembina counties.

The Germans from Russia was a more diverse group of people than the name implies or than people today think. They came from different parts of the Russian Empire; they spoke different German dialects at times influenced by Russian; they represented religious diversity: Roman Catholic, Lutheran, Baptist, Seventh Day Adventist; they developed unswerving loyalties to their respective villages or regions.

Their common experiences, however, outweighed the differences. They chafed under unsympathetic, at times hostile, governments; they faced land shortages and increasingly difficult economic times; they viewed the New World as the solution to their problems.

A Black Sea German proverb summed up their Russian experience: "For the first generation, there is death. For the second, there is want. Only for the third is there bread."

In North Dakota clearly the first generation faced hardship and heartache. But for those who toughed it out through the 1880s and 1890s (and that was most of the Germans from Russia), the good times would come for them and the second generation. The boom years, of the Golden Age of Agriculture, 1900-1920, brought unparalleled prosperity to North Dakota and the Germans from Russia.

The Children of Germans from Russia in Eureka, Dakota Territory, as pictured in the **Harper's Weekly** *feature "A Bit of Europe in Dakota," July 11, 1896. They represent the third generation that would experience the Golden Age of Agriculture in North Dakota (drawing in color on the cover).*

"Arbeit Macht das Leben Süss — "

Everett C. Albers

*G*rowing up in an island of *Reichsdeutche* in the middle of Oliver County in the heart of the German-Russian Triangle, I inherited the same brand of Lutheranism practiced in *volksdeutche* churches up in Hazen, in Mercer County. At least they were Lutheran. The German-Russian families living in the eastern part of the county, the "Rooshians," were Catholic. Neither were *really* German to the people around Hannover, North Dakota, who considered themselves better than the "Pruskies." I continue to be puzzled 50 years after I first heard about those folk so different from us *Plattdeutsche*, "Low Germans" from northern Germany.

It wasn't until I went to high school with Mosbruckers and Bobbs, Diniuses and Dolls and met and actually talked to *volksdeutsche* families living around Otter Creek, a few miles away — the Bickels, Breimeiers, Bauers and Hubers — that I found how much we had in common. Work, for one thing. *Arbeit*. Farming, German-style — whether one is of the *volksdeutsche* or *reichsdeutsche* variety, was plain old hard physical labor when both came in the 1880s and 1890s and still was when I was a boy growing up on a half-section of sub-marginal land a quarter-mile from Hannover in the 1940s and 1950s. We both lived the proverb, *"Arbeit macht das Leben süss"* — the literal translation doesn't quite carry what the short sentence means — "Work makes life sweet." Both folks around Hannover and those not-quite-really Germans lived to work instead of the other way around. Even so, we were different from each other. They worked longer and harder, started at a younger age, and continued up to the day they died if they possibly could.

Not only did they work harder, they had more fun — especially the Catholics. Their wedding dances, the *Hochzeit* ("high time"), lasted a couple of days. They polkaed and waltzed, we stood around with our hands in our pockets. When they sang in German, those who heard them for the first time found ourselves wondering whether there maybe wasn't more to music than Luther's hymns. Most amazing of all, they ate food that was a lot tastier than the meat and potatoes we were accustomed to. My *plattdeutsche* grandmothers and mother made great *kuchen*, but the *volksdeutsche* had *fleishküchla*, that glorious spiced meat rolled in dough made with sweet cream and deep fried in lard. The first time I ate one of Martha Isaak's *fleishküchlas*, I thought I had died and gone to heaven.

We were both God-fearing, but the *volksdeutsche Gott* semed to encourage more fun than ours. Moreover, they had magic. Even the most skeptical, even the most suspicious of those "Pruskies" around *reichsdeutsche* country found their way to a *volksdeutsche Brauche* woman when their backs got so out of whack that they couldn't get out of bed.

The Germans from Russia are folk of the earth. My people lived above or next to their livestock in their modest homes in northern Germany before they found their way to Illinois and Minnestoa and then to Dakota, and we have no small claim to earthiness and tuning our lives to nature. We didn't even come close to the way in which the *Volksdeutsche* took to the land. In his contribution to *Plain Folk: North Dakota's Ethnic History*, my friend Tim Kloberdanz quotes a Beulah minister, S. Joachim, in the eloquent essay on the *Volksdeutsche* he subtitles "Hungry for Land, Hungry for a Home: North Dakota's 'Other Germans'":

> The Russian German made his greatest contribution to society in the form of manual labor. By profession he is a tiller of the soil, a farmer, a producer of food. It fell to his lot to receive land in the semi-arid regions of Russia, Siberia, the Americas. . . . He built a granary out of the steppes and the prairies. He did not shout that fact to the world. A real farmer lives too close to the ground and too near to God to be a braggart. He stays humble. The dust of the earth and the smell of new-mown hay does not blear his vision.

My wife Leslie and I count among our dearest and closest friends the godparents of our son Albert and fairy godfather and godmother to our daughter Gretchen as well. Warren Henke is a *Reichsdeutcher* from New Salem — a relative of the third or fourth cousin and once-removed variety (my mother was a Henke). His wife, Rose Marie, is the granddaughter of William Fiechtner who came with his parents to Dakota from Russia when he was 19 in the year of statehood for the Dakotas, 1889. At Monango, on rocky ground, he found land and a wife, Magdalena Gebhardt, whom he wed in 1892. Among their 15 children was Rose Marie's father, Jacob Frederick, who married Rosina Kaul in 1924. Rosina passed on in July 1999 in her mid-90s. Daughter, granddaughter, great-granddaughter of *Volksdeutsche*, Rose Marie Fiechtner grew up knowing want, *"Not,"* about the same time I grew up in Hannover. Her uncle, Gottlieb Henry, and his fun-loving wife Elfrieda served the neighboring Lutheran Church-Missouri Synod in Hazen where he was pastor. She also, obviously, grew up in a home of *"Liebe,"* love. Her father died in 1945 when she was a young girl. Somehow, she and her family managed to get her to college, and she became a teacher. Rose Marie Henke loves music, cooking, sewing, and helping people. Those who tell their stories in this book often remembered the help they got from those who had come to Dakota before. Rose Marie and her husband Warren extended a welcoming hand to refugees from Ukraine in the 1990s.

Frugal and thrifty, fun-loving and loving, and as unassuming as anyone I've ever met, Rose Marie Henke is *volksdeutsche* to the marrow of her bones. She and the "Other Germans" I've come to know have done much to give us *Reichsdeutsche* a good name — their reputation has rubbed off over the last three generations. For that, we who trace our heritage to those who came directly from Germany without passing through Russia — all North Dakotans, for that matter — say *"Vielen Dank!"*

Finding an International Language

The Franz Baumgartners

/Neither party could understand the other.

Franz (born 1851) and Margaret (born 1853) Baumgartner with their five children had accompanied his brothers, Johannes and Jacobus, to America in April 1889. Franz's family separated from the other two after they arrived in Eureka and made its own way across the prairie to a homestead spot in Emmons County. Franz's story, though brief, demonstrates the ingenuity that the early settlers used to survive.

A VERY STRONG WIND SET IN as we approached our location. I immediately turned the wagon box upside down, and the entire family huddled together underneath it. The oxen were left to take care of themselves. The box served as a shelter for two days and two nights until the storm subsided.

Mr. Wallace Petrie, who lived only a mile away, was the first person to note our distress. He set out to investigate the condition of us newcomers, but neither party could understand the other as Mr. Petrie could only speak English, and I only German and Russian.

An idea came to me. I wrote my name and the reason for us being here under these conditions in

Wallace Petrie
from **A History of Emmons County**
Compiled for the Bicentennial, 1976 by the Emmons County Historical Society.

The Franz & Margaret (Thomas) Baumgartner Family
Franz was the church organist in Strassburg, Russia and later at
St. Peter and Paul's Catholic Parish in Strasburg, North Dakota
From **The Johannes Baumgartner Story and Genealogy**
Bicentennial Edition, 1774-1974.

Latin. After Mr. Petrie examined the message, he gave us the friendly signal to follow him.

We were taken to Mr. Petrie's 10- by 12-foot one-room sod shanty. Underneath the shanty was a five-foot-deep hole which he used as a cellar. His family numbered seven, including children and two relatives.

Because of the cold weather, which kept us inside, one-half of the people had to spend time in the cellar while the other half were upstairs, including meal times, when the groups ate in shifts.

Fighting the Worst of Prairie Fires

The Johannes Baumgartners

/My hayland and crop were destroyed by the fire.

Johannes was born in 1847 to Anton and Barbara Baumgartner who were first generation Germans in Strassburg, Russia. In 1867 Johannas married Margaretha Braunagel (1848) whose parents also farmed near Strassburg. The following year the couple settled on a farm not far from their parents. Before leaving for America in 1889, the Baumgartners had nine healthy children, all of whom were educated in the local Catholic church school. The Baumgartners left Russia for economic and political reasons.

AFTER A THREE-DAY TRAIN RIDE, we arrived at Eureka, Dakota Territory, which was then the western terminus of the Chicago and Milwaukee Railroad.

I purchased equipment for the farm — a pitchfork, a shovel, a plow, a wagon, two oxen, a team of horses, two cows, a kerosene stove, household supplies, and a few pieces of china and glasses.

Our family and the Jacobus Baumgartner family arrived at the Wally Petrie shanty after a two-day trip with oxen, horses, and wagon from Eureka.

We camped at the Petrie shanty that night, and with the aid of Wally Petrie and Jakob Fischer, we found our land. We moved onto a homestead two and one-half miles northwest of the village of Strasburg.

Johannes and wife Margaretha
Baumgartner in later life
above, with daughters and daughters-in-law
below, with sons and sons-in-law
From **The Johannes Baumgartner**
Story and Genealogy
Bicentennial Edition, 1774-1974.

I purchased a wagon load of boards and planks from Mr. Petrie and built an 8- by 18-foot temporary shanty. This, with the covered wagon we came in, served as our shelter until we could build a sod house, a 16- by 22-foot home we finished in June.

The walls of the house were built out of sod layers, 14 by 20 by 5 inches, overlapping each other. Inside of this wall a layer of homemade bricks was set up from the floor to the ceiling. We made the bricks from a mortar mixture of clay, prairie sod, and water, which we tramped together with our bare feet in a trough. Once these bricks were dry, we would press them out of the forms. We laid them overlapping in true brick fashion and always smeared them with a thin layer of mud. Our home was absolutely wind-proof. It served as a cool, comfortable house in the summer and a warm one during the cold season.

I vividly recollect the prairie fire of 1891 which burned for about eight days in two complete circles in and around Emmons County, from Mound City, South Dakota, to Moffit, North Dakota, a distance of 80 miles one way. The fire started two and one-half miles southeast of Westfield, North Dakota, and burned about 35 miles northwest to near Hazelton and then east about 15 miles, then south 60 miles, and then west somewhere near Herreid, South Dakota. From there it burned a stretch of prairie four miles wide up to near Temvik, North Dakota.

Fighting the Prairie Fire

"John Bartu described the firefighting equipment as being a large cow-hide which was laid flat on the ground and loaded with dirt, long wires fastened at two corners and men on horseback taking the ends of the wires, fastening them on their saddle horns, and passing over the fire to quench it to some extent. Others followed and used water-saturated sacks to beat out what fire was left. Barrels of water were hauled to the scene on stone-boats and wagons."

Text and photograph above from **A History of Emmons County** *Compiled for the Bicentennial, 1976 by the Emmons County Historical Society.*

From Temvik, it again burned east and south, completing the two cycles.

I plowed firebreaks about my farm, around my buildings. We back-fired from the breaks about 150 feet. In this way, I was able to save my buildings and household goods. My hayland and crop were destroyed. I became very sick by overworking myself and breathing the smoke-filled air.

At times, I saw the wind hurl prairie waste aflame 100 feet in the air, driving stuff ahead of the actual fire. So when the fire came to a river or firebreak, the grass would be burning on the other side before the real fire started. It was almost impossible to stop.

A Mr. Johnson and his son, who lived about one and one-half miles south of my place, were plowing firebreaks around their wheat stacks when they were suddenly overcome by smoke. They both burned to death.

As recorded in *A History of Emmons County*, edited by Ellen Woods and Euvagh Wenzel, the great fire started when a straw-burning threshing machine ignited a straw pile on September 14, 1891. Many lost their live's work. It took Harke DeBoer 17 years to pay for wheat, a new binder and wagon, and curbing for a well lost in the fire.

The fire was particularly destructive in the Holland Settlement, homes of the Dutch neighbors of the new German-Russian immigrants.

The Vander Laan children recalled "being wrapped in wet blankets and taken to a plowed field." Families drove their livestock into lakes and creeks in an effort to save their cattle and horses.

Said William Cleveringa, "Never in our lives have we seen a sight like it. It seemed that the sky was full of fire. The wind shifted three times that night. That was the worst night we ever spent. We cannot describe the awfulness."

Stealing the County Seat: Emmons County Battle

Jakob Fischer
as told by his son Mathias

They left in army style for Williamsport to haul the county safe and records to Linton.

Jacob Fischer was born in 1852 near the village of Selz in southern Russia. His parents, Carl and Margaretha, had to support 11 children on their small farm. When he was 20 years old in 1872, Jacob married Helena Ripplinger, and the couple had three children while living near Selz. Difficult economic conditions led the entire family to migrate to the United States. And, like so many Black Sea Germans, the Fischers joined with other families to make their journey. Jakob's son, Mathias, tells the story.

HAVING DECIDED, AS MANY OTHER GERMANS in the south Russia colony of Selz had done, that it was nearly impossible to make a comfortable living under the Tsar, my family made up their minds to come over to the United States of America after hearing of the many opportunities offered in America.

Jacob Jumprt the germ

7

The peasant class, to which my family belonged, was kept back so much from making progress of any kind that discouragement and agitation prevailed. So they sought new lands on which to make their livelihood.

On November 2, 1884, our troupe of immigrants arrived at New York where we remained for half a day. We took the train the same day for Yankton, Dakota Territory, a three-day trip. We were a bewildered group of people when we arrived. Each family gathered as a group around their few meager possessions. After about an hour, a Yankton citizen who acted as adviser appeared on the scene. He directed us to a hotel where we all stayed for a day.

Then the five families traveling together rented a house where they all lived for a month. Father met Martin Chamber at this time. Chamber owned a large farm with a big house on it. The five families moved into it in early December.

None of the family heads could find employment of any kind during the winter of 1884. With their funds soon exhausted, they obtained help from city and government sources.

In May 1885, father and the other families purchased two yoke of oxen, two covered wagons, and some bedding and cooking utensils. They set out for Faulk County. After a trip of 14 days, father took up a pre-emption there. In June 1886 he disposed of his rights to the land and moved to Odessa Township, Emmons County, where he homesteaded.

My father was a person of high intellectual qualities achieved through education and practical experience. He could read a surveyor's data on landmarks and section corner stones, necessary to find the land described in homesteads. He assisted many settlers in land selection. Immigrants would come to the farm and have father go along with them to help choose a claim and file the proper description.

He was elected to the Odessa School Board as a director in 1892 and served for six years. He also served continuously for eleven years on the Board of County Commissioners, once appointed, twice elected. During his first term, an unusual problem arose in Emmons County: whether or not to move the county seat to a more central location. One of three board members, father lived in the south part; the other two,

Linton in 1899

As the map below indicates, the town did not exist before the county seat was moved from Williamsport in the north part of Emmons County. The "x" above the tall building at the top of the left-most third marks the courthouse.
Photographs above and below from **A History of Emmons County**
Compiled for the Bicentennial, 1976 by the Emmons County Historical Society.
Photograph below is the Williamsport RECORD Office in 1884.

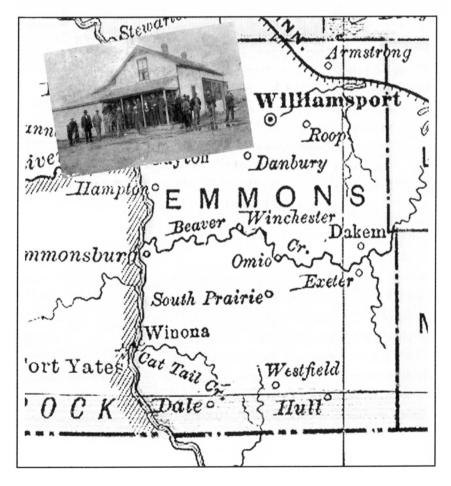

William Baxter and Alex McDonald, lived in the north part of the county.

Citizens of the south wanted the courthouse moved from Williamsport [see page 14] to the new prospective village of Linton, which lay very nearly in the middle of the county. While the three board members were at Bismarck to consult the Court about the county seat question, a group of south settlers, 200 of them, gathered at the Backhans farm two miles south of Linton. Many were on horseback, others drove wagons. They left in army style for Williamsport to haul the county safe and records to Linton, led by Charlie Patterson on a dapple-gray horse. The publisher of the *Winona Times*, he was the flag-bearer for the effort to move the county seat to Linton.

Upon their return to Williamsport, the three commissioners found that the records and safe had been stolen and taken to Linton. They returned to their homes. However, father received an order from Bismarck for the immediate return of the records to Williamsport. He borrowed an army wagon at the Backhans farm, two miles south of Linton, and loaded the safe with the help of other south county boosters. In 40-below-zero weather, they returned the records.

Father continued on to Bismarck with the bob-sleigh and horse team to present the case again to the Court. After considerable consideration, the Court granted the removal of the county seat to Linton.

His goal achieved in Bismarck, father returned to Williamsport where he delivered the judge's decision. When the other two commissioners heard the decision, they accepted in a gentlemanly manner.

Because he was the one elected from the south end of Emmons County, the job of planning the move to the new location fell to father. The records were moved into a building hurriedly erected by Charlie Patterson, who had watched very closely the entire procedure. Upon the completion of the ground floor, before the walls were up, Patterson moved his printing press and household goods into the new place of business. Linton became the county seat.

Hardship and Heartache on the Homestead

The August Flegel Family

We had come to our last crust of bread.

August Flegel was born on July 4, 1854, to Wilhelm and Carolina Flegel in the village of Kulm. Wilhelm farmed some inherited land and raised cattle, horses, sheep, and hogs. Usually the village children attended school at the Lutheran church until the age of 15. But, with 13 mouths to feed, the parents had to hire August out for farm work at an early age. His father tried to educate August at home but became disgusted with, to use August's words, "his thick-headedness." August married Christina Rieker in 1879, and the two farmed their five acres and rented land. The story of their North Dakota homestead experience reflects the serious difficulties associated with establishing a new life in a new land.

N 1885 MY WIFE'S BROTHER, JOHANNES RIEKER, became eligible for military service. The older brother Jacob was somewhat of a cripple and had been exempted from service. Johannes greatly dreaded five years in the army and decided it would be preferable to emigrate to America. He informed his parents of his decision. The thought of separation was unbearable to the parents, Ludwig and Catherine, so the entire family conferred about emigrating. My wife was easily persuaded because we had so little land of our own — and what we had was not paid for. Jacob Rieker also agreed to go.

Soon we were preparing to leave. A neighbor was offered the fuel we had on hand to advertise a sale, which he did by going from house to house ringing a bell and announcing that we would sell six horses, four or five cows, some sheep and calves, a wagon, a harrow, a plow, a table, chairs, and a cupboard. This sale netted us about 500 rubles and one of my brothers bought my land for 200 rubles [about $350 total in American money].

Finally, about the beginning of June 1889, our party — quite a large one — left Russia. Besides our family of both parents and three children — Mathilda, August Jr., and Nathanniel — there was the Ludwig Rieker family (parents and four children), the Fred Bartels (my brother-in-law, his wife, and five children), the Gottlieb Krafts with their four children, the Jacob Riekers and their children. All came from Kulm, except for the Riekers who came from Hofnungstal with the Oppermiers, the Osters, the Bauers, and three families by the name of Schlapp.

I remember in particular two incidents that happened on the journey. At the Russian border Johannes Rieker was detained on charges of desertion. The whole family remained with him pending investigation, except Jacob, who continued on with the rest of the party. About a week later the Rieker family escaped across the border after dark one night. They arrived in Dakota about a week later than the rest of us. The other incident was the sudden death of the Gottlieb Kraft infant on board the train. The body was kept secretly hidden in a woven basket until we arrived in Bremen, where it was turned over to an agent who made all necessary arrangements.

We were delayed a couple of days to await the departure of the ship from Bremen. Jacob Rieker had a problem as well, because he had depended upon his father to provide passage money. Because his father did not know how long they would be delayed at the border because of Johannes being detained, or how much money he would need to take care of the problem, he did not give Jacob enough for his passage. Jacob appealed to me. I had to tell him politely that I did not have any to spare. He then decided to ask Mr. Bartel, a relative of mine — but he didn't know him. When I told my wife of his difficulty, she said, "But what can you do? You can't leave him here." So I told Jacob I would lend him the money. His father later repaid me. I still had enough to pay my way to America, but very little else. I had intended to use the money I lent to buy stock and farm equipment, and the fact that I didn't have it caused us great suffering our first few years here.

We were aboard ship about ten days. About half-way across, the ship struck an iceberg which jarred it quite a bit and threw the passengers into a panic. Most of us became seasick, and the third-class part of the ship where we were became pretty messy. A large kettle of cooked food would be lowered, sufficient for all of us. Each helped himself or one obtained a supply large enough for his family. The food tasted rather good to those who were well, but the odor of the cooked food was terrible to those who were seasick.

Towards the end of the voyage an officer examined the passports of passengers. I had my family around me during this formality. The officer discovered that my daughter Mathilda's name was not given on the document. "And whose girl is this?" he asked. I answered that it was my daughter. "Well, her name is not given here," he replied. He threatened that, unless I paid for her passage in full, she would be returned to Bremen. I paid!

It was not a mistake that her name wasn't listed. My brother had gotten the passport for me in the hope I could save some money and had deliberately left her name out. One of the John Schlapps had a little girl the same age whose name had likewise been omitted for the same reason, but she happened to be sleeping during the examination of passports, so she was smuggled in successfully.

Upon arrival in New York, I carried two sacks containing clothing, followed by August Jr., age seven, who carried a basket containing some tools, and Mathilda, age four, who carried a little satchel containing a sad iron, and my wife, who carried little Nathanniel. After two days on the train, our family and the three Schlapp families arrived in Eureka. We were met by Fred Schott, whose wife was a cousin of my wife. The Schlapps were also related to them. Our family remained at the home of Mr. Schott for 14 days. The day after our arrival, my wife gave birth to a daughter, whom we called Magdalena. During my wife's confinement, I busied myself making a bed from some lumber. I used the left-over pieces to make a pig trough.

The First Emmons County Courthouse and Jail at Williamsport
Built in 1885 of native stone, the building cost $3,300 to construct.
from **A History of Emmons County**
Compiled for the Bicentennial, 1976 by the Emmons County Historical Society.

A friend, Mr. Kackle, who had already homesteaded in the area, contracted with me, Mr. Rieker, the three Schlapps, and a Mr. Tebele to take us to Williamsport, Emmons County, to file on land. We each paid him one dollar for his help. We arrived on the Fourth of July and found the county offices closed. Thereupon Kackle offered to take us to Bismarck for two dollars a piece more. There, he said, we would be able to obtain all the necessary papers immediately. This we agreed to, and we filed in Bismarck on July 5, 1889. When I returned to the pre-emption location, I found another family preparing to claim the land. I showed them my papers, which gave me a pre-emptor's rights, and they moved off.

Ludwig Rieker, my wife's father, built a sod house about a mile northeast of our future family home. The Rieker house was built first and a well dug there. Before it was completed, our house was begun. This was a two-room sod house about 12 by 20 feet, plastered on the outside with clay. It had two doors and four windows. One of the rooms was a small kitchen with two windows; the other was used as a dining room, parlor, and bedroom — it also had two windows. The furniture included two beds, a table and a bench, all homemade. A couple of wooden boxes were also used to sit on. Kitchen utensils consisted of a kettle and two bread pans.

We built the stoves in the house, one on either side of the partition. They were of the regular early Russian settler type, built of rock cemented with clay with a common chimney of the same material and construction. The floors were made of the same material. The walls were about six inches thick, tapering toward the top to form the chimney. An opening in the wall near the floor served as a feed door and was also used to remove the ashes.

Our food was the simplest. For breakfast my wife prepared what we called "rivel" soup out of flour and water. She rolled it to fine bits by rubbing it between the fingers, as one rubs off dough that sticks to the fingers in breadmaking. For dinner we had bread and water. The evening meal was either rivel soup or bread and water. August, our oldest, once complained, "If we only had an onion once in a while." We knew that August had detested onions in Russia, which made his complaint a truly pitiable lament. My wife sprinkled a little salt on his bread to make it taste better. Ordinarily even salt was saved for more urgent needs. I often went to the barn, knelt, and prayed. We had one cow at the time, but not for long. She soon went dry, so I decided to dispose of her. I thought that, as in Russia, in order to sell something, one had to take it to market. So I made the trip to Eureka, about 50 miles distant, with the cow. I stood on the street until evening, waiting for someone to make me an offer. About sundown a man offered to trade a wagon for the cow, and although this is not what I needed most, I made the trade.

During the first fall in 1889 I pitched grain at a threshing machine for about a month, receiving a dollar a day for my work. With these earnings I was able to purchase a few necessities for the winter. When the threshing machine finished its work in my vicinity, it was moved to Bowdle. Because I was a fast and hard worker, I was the only one of its pitchers to be asked to go along with the machine. When I was told that the pitchers would have to sleep in the straw stacks, and since it was beginning to get quite cold, I refused the offer.

The next three years brought crop failures. They were very hard years for us. In the summer time I worked occasionally for a Hollander

Main Street of Eureka, Dakota Territory, in the Early Years
From **Eureka: 1887-1937**, *a publication of Eureka's Golden Jubilee Organization in 1937 which was edited by the Federal Writer's Project of the Works Progress Administration.*

neighbor, Mr. Tone Ver Hoeven. I plowed and did other odd jobs. My wife also worked there doing washing, ironing, and mending. For our services we received such articles as salt, sugar, meat, old clothing, and, occasionally, a loaf of bread or cup of rice. In this way, we kept the family alive.

In the fall of 1890, Mr. Ver Hoeven had no more work for me and was unable to extend me any more aid. Because I could not get work of any kind near home because of the crop failure, I decided to leave home to try to find work somewhere else. I said goodbye to my family, and, in the company of my father-in-law, set out afoot across the prairies. For more than a month the family heard nothing of me and did not know whether I was alive or dead. I got work 15 miles south of Eureka for a month. We labored from early morning to late at night, slept in a manger, and at the end of the month received $12. We were asked to continue, but I thought the salary too meager. I was also homesick, so our employer took me as far as Eureka one morning. I arrived home about dusk after walking the rest of the way.

Later, during this same fall of 1890, after the $12 was used up, we found ourselves in great distress again. I had acquired a few necessities — a team of oxen, a wagon, a plow, and a few cows and calves. But everything was mortgaged. I went to town with Mr. Ver Hoeven and tried to get some flour on credit. All dealers refused because I could not give them a first mortgage on my chattels. On the way home I felt very badly, and Mr. Ver Hoeven suggest that he mortgage one of his steers and obtain flour that way. I accepted with the understanding that the animal was to remain the property of Ver Hoeven. I obtained 100 pounds of flour this way, but I was unable to pay when the note was due. Ver Hoeven, fearing he might lose his steer, butchered it and told me to say that it had died. The mortgager put the matter in the hands of a lawyer for collection, who charged eight dollars for his fee, which I thought exorbitant. I remonstrated with the lawyer saying, "*Was recht ist hat Gott lieb* [God loves what is right]." The lawyer purposefully misunderstood me and replied, laughingly, in German, "Your name is August, not Gottlieb."

The next fall, that of 1891, after another crop failure, was another period of destitution for us. We came to our last crust of bread, which my wife divided among the children. She and I had nothing. After their supper, we washed the children and put them to bed. We then retired to the other room where I took down the Bible, read a passage, and then we knelt down and petitioned our Heavenly Father for help. The next day Reverend Hilscher of Eureka Evangelical Church arrived with the announcement that flour and clothing had arrived in Eureka for distribution to the needy. I and my father-in-law were soon on our way. I obtained 900 pounds of flour and some clothing. The best of the clothes had already been taken, however; and my wife burned what I brought home because it was absolutely unfit to wear.

The first couple of years our children could not attend school because they had no clothes. We were so poor that the children wore old clothes on their feet for shoes. About 1891 they tried to go to school, but even then their clothing seemed ridiculous to the other children, who made fun of them. It became the practice of our children to gather their clothing and dinner pails during the last recess and to rush from school as soon as dismissed by teacher and run home as fast as they could. If they were unsuccessful in this attempt, they remained at school until the last of their tormenters had gone home. We finally protested to the teacher, and schooldays became a little more bearable for our children.

We lived about three years on the pre-emption. About 1892, unable to prove up [pay for it], I took a homestead and lived there about seven years and proved up. I also bought a quarter from the railroad on terms that gave me ten years to pay. With better times I paid for it in less time and lived there until 1908.

The year we moved from the pre-emption to the homestead, I bought a team of horses for $550. I was swindled, because neither horse amounted to much. I paid interest and a small amount on the principle each year. Finding this method of payment rather expensive, I determined to pay in full in 1897. I sold seven head of cattle and three horses and turned the proceeds over, but I was still about $25 short. By the time I paid for the team, the horses cost me over $700.

About this time I also bought another smaller horse from Henry Van Soest for $25. To pay for it, I agreed to build a sod house for Van Soest. My wife and I worked on this barn together for three weeks, so our pay was about 50 cents a day. My wife had an infant child, Fred, whom she took along to work. Mathilda also came along to take care of the baby.

In 1897 our family was cast in deep sorrow by the death of our oldest son and brother, August. On June 30th of that year a dark cloud came up in the western sky late in the afternoon. I told my two boys, August, age 15, and Nathanniel, age 10, to pick up the horses. My wife was baking bread, and August loved freshly baked bread. He lingered a while, hoping to get a slice before doing his work. His mother told him to tend to the horses; when he came back, she would give him a slice of bread. I was helping Nathanniel drive the stakes when we heard a loud crash. I was stunned a little while. When I came to myself, I looked around and saw that the horse August was leading was lying down. I went over to look and found August lying underneath, killed by a bolt of lightning.

When a Volksdeutsche Marries a Reichsdeutcher

Minnie Sperling Freitag

We were hungry when we went to sleep and hungry when we woke up.

Born on June 10, 1879, in the village of Mansburg, Bessarabia, to John and Louise Sperling, Minnie, not yet six years old, accompanied her parents to America in 1886. Her father, whom she describes as "very progressive," left Russia because he became "very dissatisfied with the political situation." Unlike most German-Russian women, she did not marry within that ethnic group. She did, however, wed a third-generation German-American, A.J. Freitag, who was born at Wayside, Wisconsin, in 1871. He worked as a salesman and later opened a hardware store in Kulm.

E WERE 35 DAYS ON OUR JOURNEY from the time we left Russia until we landed at Scotland, Dakota Territory. When we arrived at New York we had one dollar cash. That was all we had to live on for the five days it took us to complete our journey. We would get two small loaves of bread a day and divide them among the six of us. There was nothing to go with the bread except water. We were hungry when we went to sleep and hungry when we woke up. The family

North Dakota in 1893 — Kulm Circled

Inserted photograph included Minnie's brother Dave, lying down, left center.

Photograph from **Kulm Diamond Jubilee, Supplement to 1957 Jubilee Book,**
a publication of The Kulm Messenger, 1967.

had three cents left in cash when we arrived in Scotland, Dakota, where we had relatives who received us.

One of the first things my father did was to apply for citizenship. He always took an active part in politics. He was a dyed-in-the-wool Democrat.

In the spring of 1886 we moved to Ellendale, Dakota Territory. This town was called the "End of the World" because it was at the end of the railroad tracks. Father filed on a homestead and pre-emption 40 miles northwest of Ellendale in Antelope Valley in McIntosh County.

Our first shelter at our homestead was a hole in the ground with our wagon box tipped over it. We lived there until we built our house. The only lumber we used for construction was for the door, window, frame, and table. For the roof we got some poles from the coulee and covered them with sod.

We built our stove out of clay, partly in the house and partly out. It was fired from the outside. We used it for six years. For fuel we used slough grass, prairie (buffalo) chips, and, mostly, manure — which we prepared in the summer for winter use. Most of the settlers did not know what kind of fire coal would make. They couldn't use coal in the clay ovens anyway. *Oxaleen* was the name of the fuel they used, the most important fuel for the first 20 years.

We started farming by breaking the land with oxen and plow. We had no crop for the first two years, no rain in the summer months. Our only income came from picking buffalo bones. We hauled them to Ellendale where we received $7 a ton. It would take four days to make the trip, and we would let the oxen graze on the way. We made about four trips a year until we finally raised a crop. Later the Soo Line was built to Monango, much closer to us than Kulm, only ten miles away.

The first year on the homestead all we had to live on was bread, milk, and cheap coffee, and it all tasted very good. For the Christmas holidays we would buy a sack of fine flour, and it would have to last for the whole year for baking coffee cake for Sundays. The second year on our homestead we had enough vegetables. That made life more complete. We only put sugar on the table when the pastor visited our home. Our grocery bill for a whole year would amount to less than $25.

When father bought our first binder, the dealer obtained a preliminary mortgage on the homestead without father's knowledge. When we proved up on the homestead, the dealer took the homestead, binder and all, and chased us off. The price of the binder may have been $110. We then moved to our pre-emption. This was in 1893. After that we started getting a fair break.

Sonya

The Men of Kulm
Bottom, Dave (Minnie's Brother)
Very top, Minnie's Husband,
A.J. Freitag
(See page 20 for photo credit.)

The first year we arrived in the United States, when I was seven, my parents hired me out to a farm family as a nursemaid. I took care of children and lugged them around — they were about as heavy as I was. As a salary for a year's work I received a pair of shoes, a pair of stockings, an apron, a calico dress, a hat, and two small, six-week-old pigs — which were given to my parents.

The second year I was again hired out as a nursemaid. My oldest brother, Dave, worked at the same place. We worked for the entire year for two steers that my father got to use as oxen the year before.

After that, I stayed with my parents on the farm where I herded cattle, dug stones, and hoed the garden until I was confirmed in 1895. Then I took up hotel work in Kulm until 1898. I followed that up with the dress-making trade until 1901. On March 3, I married A.J. Freitag, a hardware merchant in Kulm.

Late in 1901 we sold our interests in Kulm and entered into partnership with my husband's brother, H.R. Freitag, in the general mercantile and implement business in Velva, where we stayed until 1906, when we sold and homesteaded near Max.

Searching for Good Land in Logan County

Johann Gutschmidt

Everybody was, by 1888, talking of leaving Russia . . .

Christoph and Rosina Opp Gutschmidt owned a small wheat farm near the village of Denovitz just as their parents had. In 1864 Johann was born, and when he became seven years old, he attended school where both German and Russian languages were used in instruction. When he graduated at age 15, he went to work for his father on the farm. After he married Rosina Opp in 1886, the newlyweds lived with the senior Gutschmidts and received a small share of the crop for their farm work. Because the farm was too small to support two families, they all decided to leave for America.

EVERYBODY WAS, BY 1888, talking of leaving Russia and going to America. Young men did not seem to have any chance for the future. Many of the people from our village of Denovitz had already settled in America, among them John and George Weispfenning, K.A. Kruger, Michael Brost, and Daniel Netz. All of them except Netz had settled in Logan County, Dakota Territory. They wrote occasional letters to friends and neighbors in Denovitz which kept me interested in and aroused my desire to join them. My father and his family also decided to go, so we made the trip together. Father sold the farm to

Johann Miller and Jacob Fischer. The whole family prepared: I and my wife and our eight-month-old daughter, Lydia; my brothers, Jacob and Christoph; my sisters, Caroline and Mary; and my parents. We toasted bread and dried meat and also cooked milk and put it into tightly sealed jars for the journey.

On May 19, 1889, we traveled by wagon to Leipzig, Russia, where we boarded a train for Bremen, Germany. We had to go on the ship as steerage passengers because we did not have very much money. We suffered from the usual seasickness, but not to excess; and we docked at New York City nine days after boarding. On June 3, 1889, we arrived by train at Edgeley, Dakota Territory [see map, page 20].

We didn't know anyone when we arrived, and as none of us could speak English, we were quite worried about finding out where to go. It just so happened that, on the day of our arrival in Edgeley, two boys, John and Daniel Fercho from the King Settlement (Township 134, Range 69, Logan County) were in town to get some supplies. They were also natives of Russia, and they helped us establish ourselves. I wanted to go as far as the German settlement north of Fredonia, and the Fercho boys took us to the Weispfenning homestead where we stayed until we could build a house on our claim.

I started at once to look for a good piece of land. The soil was rich, and plenty of rain fell, so farming was good. I decided on the NE¼, Section 2, Township 133, Range 67 in Logan County, about 20 miles west of Edgeley and two miles east of the Weispfenning homestead. There was quite a settlement of German-Russians there.

I started building our home on June 10th or 12th. It took me 14 days to complete our first house of sod, 16 by 20 feet. There were only two rooms, a bedroom and a kitchen. We had one door and three windows. The walls were of sod with a coating of clay, the roof of sod laid on rough boards.

I had $250 left when I arrived in America, and I was careful with that money because I did not know if I would be able to earn more. I bought cheap boards to make some benches, a table, two beds, shelves, and a clothes closet. We bought some kitchen utensils and only such food as was absolutely necessary because flour cost $1.50 to $1.75, sugar about $4.00 per hundred, and Arbuckle coffee $1.00 for eight

Johann Gutschmidt

A More Comfortable Home
This one in Emmons County used
lumber as well as sod for the walls.
It is twice the size of most
German-Russian settlers' first houses.
From **A History of Emmons County**
Compiled for the Bicentennial, 1976 by
the Emmons County Historical Society.

pounds. We moved into our house late in June. About four years later I built a more comfortable house.

We had no well at the farm at first, and for the first few weeks we had to use slough water for household use. Later, I dug a shallow well near a slough, and the water was somewhat cleaner. There was plenty of water in the slough for my stock.

After a few weeks on the homestead, I decided to buy a team of oxen so that I would not be dependent on my neighbors so much. Charles Schields, a general store and implement dealer in Edgeley, extended me credit to buy the oxen and purchase flax seed, a wagon, and a plow. I traded my sheepskin coat to get my first cow. We bought some wool so my wife could spin it and knit our garments. I made a little money by working for neighbors and picking buffalo bones to sell in Edgeley for about $2 a wagon load.

In the fall of 1889 a huge prairie fire swept the settlement, a new experience for us. We had never seen such a sight. The grass was about a foot high and very dense, so once a fire started, it was hard to put out. We quickly plowed a good firebreak around the farm, so the fire did us no damage.

We had not counted on the hard winters. The winters in Russia were comparatively mild; and to me, it hardly seemed possible that a winter could be so severe and last so long. The snow came in October and stayed until April or May. We did, however, come through our first winter with good health and spirits. We spent most of the time at home, except for visits with the neighbors and attending church services at each other's homes. Occasionally the men had to go to Edgeley, and we went as a group when we did so we could break a better road through the deep snow. The round trip could take four days.

Plowing with Oxen
Most of the first settlers did not ride in comfort,
for they usually could afford no more than a walking plow.
Photograph from the Elwyn B. Robinson Department of Special Collections,
Chester Fritz Library, Unversity of North Dakota, Grand Forks, N.D.

In the spring of 1890, I broke my first land, 20 acres which I seeded to flax. Even though it was quite dry, I harvested 135 bushels. Flax sold for about 90 cents a bushel, so I was able to pay off the year's debts.

In 1895 we in the area built the first schoolhouse and a church. Most of us were Lutheran, so we called the church St. John's Lutheran Church. We built it for $800 — a frame building about 22 by 28 feet with neither a steeple nor a bell. We paid our first minister $500 a year.

Sod Church in Tripp County, South Dakota
Many of the first churches on the Dakota prairie had neither steeple nor
bell — they were often made of the same material settlers used for their
houses. The one above is a Methodist church.
Fred Hultstrand History in Pictures Collection, NDIRS-NDSU, Fargo, N.D.

Homesteading, Pre-empting, and Tree Claiming in Dickey County

Simon Hille

I thought I was in another world.

Daniel Hille, who had left Russia in 1874 to homestead near Scotland, Dakota Territory, convinced his younger brother, Simon (born March 29, 1868), to migrate to America before his 18th birthday to avoid service in the Russian army. So, eleven days before his birthday, March 18, 1886, Simon Hille began his journey to Dakota in the company of several families from Bessarabia in southern Russia. His parents, Gottlieb and Wilhelmina, felt bad about their son's leaving but knew that America offered him a brighter future. Gottlieb gave Simon $175 for the journey.

OUR PARTY LANDED AT CASTLE GARDEN on the 6th day of April, 1886. A minister who represented the steamship company took charge of all of the passengers on the ship *Elba* and guided us to a hotel in New York City, where we all had a good meal. I thought I was in another world. The trains were larger and more comfortable, the food was better, and the people treated us better and were more polite than in Europe. The American people were kinder than the Russians, and they wanted immigrants to settle in the United States.

Seven Coaches of German-Russian Emigrants Arrive in Eureka
The exodus continued throughout the 1890s —
the photograph above was taken in 1892.
Photograph from **Eureka: 1887-1937,** *a publication of Eureka's Golden Jubilee*
Organization in 1937 which was edited by the Federal Writer's Project
of the Works Progress Administration.

The minister representing the steamship company took our party to the railway station; and, after we gave our destination, address, and names of relatives waiting for us in Dakota Territory, he purchased our railroad tickets. Of course we had to pay for the tickets, but the minister saw to it that everything was done right.

We changed trains in Chicago and from there went directly to Scotland, Dakota Territory. We purchased lunch in New York and Chicago and fruit in the larger towns on the route. We slept on the seats in the train coaches. It took four days via railroad to make the trip at a cost of about $150. We arrived April 10, 1886.

When I left Russia, I wrote my brother, Daniel, who lived near Scotland, that I was coming to the United States. He did not know the exact date when I would arrive because of the delays in Europe and in transferring from one train to another. Most fortunately, when we arrived in Scotland, he and his wife happened to be at an elevator cleaning flax. I located him; and, after the flax was cleaned, we went out to his homestead. The rest of the group went in several directions, either with friends or relatives, to settle on favorable land.

I worked for my brother on his farm from April 1886 to January 1887, nine months, for which he paid me $25. But he also seeded 15 acres of flax for me, from which I realized only seven bushels. After it was threshed, there was a load of flax straw which I sold in Scotland for $8.

The winter of 1886-87 was very cold with much snow on the ground. We did not have any recreation during the winter because neighbors were so scarce. However, we spent our spare time reading the Bible and a German newspaper, The *Dakota Freie Presse*. We men spent a lot of  time currying Daniel's horses because he was very particular about them — everything had to be just so. His horses were kept in excellent condition.

After leaving Daniel's farm in January 1887, I worked for Adam Mey, a settler living three miles north of Lesterfield, Dakota Territory. I did farm work there for a year, through January 1888, for which I received $130 in wages. For recreation, we read during that bad winter. Blizzards were numerous, the snow very deep. It was also cold, but no one in the vicinity froze to death.

During January-February 1888, I was employed by the Milwaukee Railroad Company at $1.50 per day shoveling snow off the tracks between Tindle and Scotland. On March 1, 1888, I hired out to an old Englishman, Peter Devore, a fifty-year-old who did not know anything about farming. He lived six miles southwest of Scotland. I had to show and teach him how to farm. I spent ten months there and received $12 a month in pay. While there, I learned how to speak English, but I could not learn to write in English — I couldn't grasp the fundamentals of writing English letters.

After leaving the Devore farm, I found work on the Ludvig Doerring homestead, located about ten miles north of Tripp, between that town and Parkston. I took care of Doerring's stock. While in this vicinity I met Susan Hille, daughter of Johann Hille, whose farm was seven miles south of Parkston. We were wed on February 19, 1889, in Tripp and lived with her parents for about three weeks after the wedding.

About this time I met Nathaniel Leischner, who rented a farm ten miles southeast of Parkston. He was married as well, but he did not have children. He and I decided to leave the area because there was no land to be taken up. On March 9, 1889, he and I rented a railroad car from the Milwaukee Railroad Company in Parkston. I had received two cows and a pig from my wife's parents. My brother-in-law, Gottlieb Sprecher, gave us a bunch of small trees to use in case we filed a tree claim. I bought two colts for $75 and a second-hand wagon on credit and two oxen for $110. We also had some bedding and clothes. Leischner had four horses, two cows, one wagon, bedding, some clothes, and a small supply of feed.

The Milwaukee Railroad Company only allowed one person in a boxcar to take care of the livestock and get free fare. We decided I would be the one. Leischner was short of money and was going to take a chance on riding in the boxcar with me. Our wives were riding in the passenger coaches. Every once in a while, during the trip from Parkston to Edgeley, a brakeman would open the door and ask me if there was anything I needed, asked me how I was getting along. As soon as the car door began to open, Leischner would duck among the horses and oxen and hide. After this happened several times, he was covered with manure and looked a sight. He earned his fare, all right, by being scared and dirty.

The trip to Edgeley took a day and one-half. We arrived on March 11, 1889. The United States afforded opportunities to take up land and gave us a chance to make a fair living. The country around Edgeley was not so thickly settled, but we didn't care. We stayed in town overnight. We put the stock up at a livery barn and drew the wagons up beside it. We put the rest of our belongings in a store owned by Mr. Kesler.

On March 12, 1889, we traveled to Whitestone Township, Dickey County, a trip of about a day to a place 25 miles southwest of Edgeley. The Leischners went to the Koenig settlement, 12 miles north of Lehr.

First House in Monango, 1887
There was not much in the town when Simon Hille first visited, but within a
couple of years Monango was booming. The railroad bypassed nearby
Keystone, three miles away. In the winter of 1886-87, sled runners were put
beneath buildings in Keystone, which were hauled to the new railroad site
created by the Milwaukee Railroad at Monango. By 1909, Monango was the
busy community in the photograph on the next page.
Photographs courtesy of Don Frigen.

We went to my brother-in-law's (Jacob Medche) homestead eight miles southwest of Kulm. We stayed there for five weeks while I searched for land. Medche had a sod house with two large rooms and an entry. He had many children, so there was congestion while we were there. Some of the children had to sleep on the floor, and sometimes we nearly walked over each other. However, the food was good, and the house was clean. We made the best of it and did not suffer any.

I took up three claims in the township, filing on a homestead, pre-emption, and a tree claim ten miles south of Kulm — all in the same section of land. I went the 32 miles to Ellendale to file my three claims. We built a sod shack 12 by 14 feet on the pre-emption claim. It had one room, one window, and one door. We lived in this shack for six months. In the meantime, we built a 16- by 24-foot sod house on our homestead. It had two rooms and a large entry, four windows and two doors. I built a stove out of lime bricks into the wall which partitioned off the two rooms for cooking and heat. We used twisted hay and prairie waste for fuel.

I went the 18 miles to Monango and purchased the following on credit: one hand plow, a drag, and a hay mower. With my team of oxen and the hand plow, I broke 20 acres of land and seeded it to flax. I didn't realize a single bushel because it was too dry that year. To make a living in 1889, I stacked hay and sold it. During the fall and winter of 1889-1890 I hauled 18 loads of hay to Monango where I sold it for $7 or $8 per load. We used the money to buy food and clothes that year.

I was able to hold all three claims. I grew ten acres of trees the first year to secure my tree claim. To hold the pre-emption, I had to pay $240. To hold the homestead we had to live on it for five years. We were fortunate enough to pay for the pre-emption.

A Mr. Haggerty, who lived in Monango, operated the Keystone Loan Company, which was supposed to help finance pre-emption claims made by settlers who did not have the necessary money at the time their payments were due. The main objective of the company, however, was to get title to the homesteads. Mr. Haggerty wanted a mortgage on both the pre-emption and the homestead. When settlers who had mortgaged both finally had enough money to pay off the pre-emption, they found that their homesteads were still mortgaged. Mr. Haggerty refused to give back the title to the homestead because he claimed it was a separate matter not connected to the pre-emption. In this manner many settlers had their homesteads stolen from them.

good
Sub-Plot

The Banker gets slot

Monango in 1909

From Bessarabia to Northern Dakota: A Family's Journey

The Gottlieb Isaak Family

We thought that we were very lucky and that this was heaven.

Christian and Wilhelmina Isaak farmed near the village of Kulm in the Bessarabia region of southern Russia. Christian also did blacksmith work. On July 16, 1860, their sixth of seven children was born; they named him Gottlieb. Between the ages of six and fifteen Gottlieb attended school — German in the morning, Russian in the afternoon. School ended because he had to help his father in his work. In 1881 he married Christina Beich, and the two farmed near Kulm for two years. They moved to Gnadenfelt where they eked out a living on the land for five years. There the couple had two children. Excited by letters from America that told of free land and a happier life, and fearing a draft into the Tsar's army, Gottlieb made the momentous decision: off to America!

N **THE FIRST PART OF APRIL 1886,** I and my wife Christina, our children, Mathilda and Otto; my parents, Christian and Wilhelmina Isaak; and my younger brother, Gottfried, decided to go to America. We took along only clothing, bedding, and some money. We traveled by rail to Hamburg, Germany, a trip of three days. At Hamburg we secured passage on a steamship bound for America. It took us twelve days to cross the Atlantic Ocean. The accommodations were bad, the food hardly fit to eat, and the sleeping quarters were musty and had odors. The voyage was a rough one; several storms slowed down the progress of the trip.

We landed in Baltimore, Maryland, the last part of April. We liked the looks of everything we saw when we landed. We thought that we were very lucky and that this was heaven. The people treated us much better than in Russia and were more civilized. The American trains were larger, twice-again as long as the Russian and European trains. The food in America was better and just as cheap in price.

That same night we boarded a train bound for Dakota Territory. At Chicago, Illinois, we changed trains. We went straight to Scotland, Dakota Territory. I, my father and my brother Gottfried slept in the aisles of the train coaches from Baltimore to Scotland in order to make it easier for the women and children, who slept in the seats. Many times the conductors had to step over our bodies in order to walk through the train. The train men did not like this very much, but they did not object because, as they told us, it could not be helped because of our poverty.

We reached Scotland on May 5, 1886. The cost of the trip from our Russian home to Scotland was about 300 Russian rubles, about $150 in American money. I had 35 cents in American coin left in my pockets. The trip for all of us was so cheap due to the pass rule the steamship companies and railroads had in effect at that time: all children who accompanied their parents on railroads or on a sea voyage, regardless of age, were allowed to travel free of charge.

August Schultz, who knew us in south Russia where he was a very good friend, met us at the depot in Scotland. Mr. Schultz had come to America about five years before. He took us to his farm, about 22 miles north of Scotland — a trip of about four hours. He had a sod house and other buildings made of lumber; they were better than on Russian farms.

At first I did not like the country because I could not speak English, and the country was strange to me. My older brother, Johann, who had come to America in 1877, had homesteaded about ten miles west of the Schultz farm. We went to his place next. His farm was fair. The house was constructed of lumber; it was a two-story building. There was a

Typical Modest Sod House in Dakota
Fred Hultstrand History in Pictures Collection, NDIRS-NDSU, Fargo, N.D.

summer kitchen which stood alone. There was plenty of room for everyone.

My brother, Gottlieb, got a job on a farm near Parkston [see map, page 20]. He earned 75 cents a day for working in the harvest fields and helping with the threshing.

I was employed on the Johann Leischner farm, located twelve miles east of my brother's homestead. I worked there all summer in the hay and harvest fields and worked on threshing machines that fall. I also earned 75 cents per day. My parents, wife, and two children lived with Johann, making their home in the summer kitchen.

During the winter of 1886-87, we continued to live with Johann. There were heavy falls of snow that winter, many storms; and it was very cold most of the time. I was much colder than I was in winter in Russia. Our social activity during that winter was visiting neighbors and having talkfests with them.

My brother, Gottfried, met and was united in marriage with Caroline Leischner, a daughter of the farmer for whom he worked. The wedding took place in the spring of 1887, and the couple took up a homestead 25 miles east of Parkston.

During the first part of May 1887, our family decided to travel northward because there was no more land in the Scotland vicinity to be taken up or bought. I went to a neighbor of my brother, whose name was Daniel Grosz. I borrowed $100 from him to help finance our trip. He said I could pay it back as I saw fit to do so. With the money I had earned in the summer and fall of 1886, I purchased a team of oxen for $70. I bought a wagon and a plow. Because I wanted to have some money on hand, I used some of my credit to purchase a team of ponies for $125.

In the company of the Ludwig and Michael Henneberg families, we hired a boxcar at Parkston and loaded our wagons, horses, oxen and farm implements in it. One person was allowed to travel free of charge in this car. Michael wanted to ride the car, so we allowed him to do so. The rest of us traveled in the passenger cars. We families arrived in Ellendale one and one-half days later.

In open wagons drawn by horses and oxen, we began to move west, and in one day arrived at the homestead of Andrew Schadler, a settler who lived about 35 miles northwest of Ellendale. After remaining the night, the Hennebergs left and traveled south about seven miles where both families took up homesteads and tree claims.

In the first part of June, I and my father went to Hoskins to file for land. I both homesteaded and filed a tree claim; my father filed just a tree claim. My homestead land was in McIntosh County, Antelope Township, the NE¼ of Section 12. My tree claim was in German Township, Dickey County, the SW¼ of Section 6. Father's tree claim was in the SE¼ of the same section.

I built a 16- by 16-foot sod house on my homestead with the help of my father. My parents intended to live with us. We bought lumber for the walls and roof in Ellendale for $7 — lumber for support, because the house was made of lime, clay, and sod. It had one room, five windows and two doors. A year later we added two rooms. We all lived in this house for eight years.

That first year I broke about ten acres of land. With so much available hay on my homestead and tree claim, I thought it would be profitable to make hay that summer. I purchased a hay mower and rake from an implement dealer in Ellendale on credit. I stacked the hay. I figured I would have no trouble selling it in Ellendale where there were many livery barns. I made a hay rack of lumber bought in Ellendale, and in the winter of 1886-87 when our food supply got low, I would load a big rackful of hay and take it to Ellendale with my oxen. There I would sell it for $7 to $10 per ton. I made many tons of hay that summer and fall. In Ellendale I was allowed to sleep in the mercantile store. In the morning I would buy supplies and return home. That how I made a living for us in 1887-88.

I also earned money picking buffalo bones. The bones were becoming more scarce with the passing of each month, so I had to cover quite a bit of territory to gather a double wagon box full of bones. In the middle of July 1887 I hitched my team of ponies to the wagon. I was about 30 miles north of my homestead, and the wagon was nearly full. All of a sudden, one of the ponies became sick and lay down on the ground. I was lucky that there was a slough with some water in it nearby. Taking a pail which I carried at all times, I filled it. After an hour, the pony revived, and I could start for home. I let the ponies take their time, so it was a long journey; but I reached home without walking or the pony becoming sick again.

I and my father started the 35-mile trip to Ellendale one morning in the latter part of November 1887. Our food supply was becoming very low, and we wanted to get more stock before severe weather set in. As there was very little snow, we traveled to Ellendale in a wagon drawn with our team of oxen. The weather was fair, not very cold. We reached the village and stayed overnight. In the morning we bought our supplies and started for home. The weather was calm and clear, but a little cold. After traveling about 15 miles the weather suddenly turned, and it began to snow. It turned colder, the snow got thicker. The sun disappeared, and it was getting darker. We traveled five more miles before the oxen played out. The beasts lay on the snow and would not get up. The snow was piling up, and it was nearly impossible to continue with the wagon. We were very cold because the clothing my father and I had on was not very warm.

Sod Buildings on the Frontier in the Winter
From the Fred Hultstrand History in Pictures Collection, NDIRS-NDSU, Fargo, N.D.

We were most fortunate that close by, about one-fourth of a mile, there stood a couple of small buildings. We unhitched the oxen and took them with us to these buildings. We found that the small, one-room shanty and the barn were locked. A Mr. Kalbaus, a bachelor, lived here during the spring, summer, and fall, but went east during the winter. We broke open the padlocks, and, after we had our oxen safely in the barn and had given them hay from the wagon, we went into this small shanty. We found some coal, tea, and a little canned goods. Mr. Kalbaus kept the coal on hand for the chilly days during the fall. After we started a fire in the small stove, we cooked the tea and had a meager meal. We slept in the bunk that night.

Looking out of one of the two windows the next morning, we saw deep snow, which was very loose. Traveling with the wagon would be impossible. Being something of a carpenter, I found some lumber, a hammer, nails, ropes, and some leather in the barn. I made a crude sled. We hitched the team of oxen to it and started for home. We traveled about six miles when the sled broke down, making it impossible to go farther. It was bitterly cold now. I told my father to remain with the sled and animals while I walked to the farm of Johann Lay, about four miles southwest of our sled.

It was a clear day, as it had quit snowing. By the time I reached the Lay homestead, I was nearly frozen. Gottlieb Lay, a son of Johann Lay, hitched four horses to one of their sleds and drove to our sled. Father was on the verge of freezing. With great difficulty, the Lays pulled us home.

A Sunny Day After the Blizzard
Fred Hultstrand History in Pictures Collection,
NDIRS-NDSU, Fargo, N.D.

The next spring, I went to the Kalbaus homestead to get my wagon. I asked him if any robbers had been to his place that winter. He told me that somebody was there and had broken open the locks, but he thought it was travelers who had occupied his shanty and barn. I told him that it was I who had been there and related the entire story of that trip. I told him I was there to get my wagon. I also asked what I owed him for the lumber and other materials I used to make the crude sled. Mr. Kalbaus refused to take anything. He said he was only glad that we did not freeze to death.

I had good crops all the years I was on the farm. My first crop in 1886 yielded about 125 bushels from ten acres. I had purchased a binder in Ellendale, on credit, and harvested the wheat with this machinery. A neighbor, John Lay, threshed for me. Profit from sales at 90 cents a bushel helped pay for a new small barn.

In 1896 we decided to build a new house, so I rented about five acres of land from a neighbor for $15. About half of the house would be homemade from bricks, and my neighbor's land had good clay on it. In the spring, my whole family began work. I plowed up the clay, which had considerable lime mixed in with it. We scraped out the clay with oxen and put it in a pile. We used barrels to haul water from the slough to the pile. We poured the water over the mixture and left it to soften for a day. We hauled straw from my pile and mixed it in, about half a load to mix one batch. Homemade bricks would not hold together without the straw.

A Prosperous German-Russian Dakota Farmer
The home pictured above, like the one Gottlieb Isaak had a brickmaker construct for him, had walls a foot and one-half thick, In this case, the homemade bricks were whitewashed. Not only were such homes warm in the winter and cool in the summer, they were virtually fireproof.
Photograph from **Harper's Weekly**, *July 11, 1896.*

While the bricks were left to dry and harden for two and one-half months, we harvested and threshed our crop. I found a bricklayer in Kulm. He worked for one week, at $2 a day. We built a six-room, two-story house, three rooms upstairs and three rooms downstairs. The walls were about eighteen inches thick. We bought lumber, plaster, and shingles to complete the house in Kulm. We didn't dig a basement, but did make a small cellar.

My parents passed away in the new house, father in 1897, mother in 1898. Katherine and I had seven children born on the homestead.

Jacobs wife got hurt while pregnat
+
was burren afta wards -

Looking for Water: From the Hague Settlement to Buffalo Lake

Max Keller

"My garsh!" D thought, "is this the North Pole?"

Max Keller was born in 1854 on his parents' (Wilhelm and Katerina) small farm 40 miles northwest of Odessa, at Monheim near the Black Sea. From age six on, Max helped his parents with the farm work. In 1881 Max married Julianna Webber, and the couple had three children: Anton (1885), Katerina (1881), and Magdalena (1887). The Kellers left Russia to escape, in Max's words, "a terrible struggle." Their destination was Hague in Emmons County, a settlement where many German-Russians had homesteaded. Max's father Wilhelm toughed it out during the dry years, but not Max. Demonstrating the German-Russian inclination toward moving on to a better place, after seven years Max relocated his family in Pierce County where more water was available.

*M*Y FATHER HAD BEEN TALKING ABOUT going to America off and on for many years, but it seemed that it was next to impossible to save enough money at any one given time to meet the expense of the trip. As times became harder and the work more severe, he decided that something had to be done to get to a better land, and that land was to be America! Therefore, the family as a whole decided to use every means possible to save and economize in the hope of eventually being able to emigrate.

After a long period of saving, it was finally possible. Happy was the day when we got together and summed things up and found that we could all go. On the first day of March 1889, I, my wife, our three children, and my parents started from Monheim, Russia. After considerable difficulty we succeeded in getting across the border to Germany. We had been told that the watchman at the border would have to be bribed, which we were prepared to do in the manner described by those who went before us — having a coin in your hand that was slipped to the guard just as you crossed the border, while he was pretending to read your pass. But when we came, there were other officers present who expected to be bribed too. We did not understand this at first, so we were stopped by those other officers. It soon dawned on us that they wanted to be bribed as well. So we handed them coins in a way no one saw, and they permitted us to go. We arrived at Bremen in Germany the third day, and there we boarded a boat that was to go directly to New York City. When I saw them raise the large anchor and the boat being towed to deeper water, I was so glad. At last we were on our way to that great country about which we had all heard so much good. When I looked about me, I noticed that I was not alone in my smile of satisfaction. All about me stood men, women, and children shouting: "We are going; we are on our way to America!"

After the boat got out to sea aways, we started talking with the passengers, and I found that same feeling existed among all of them. They were glad that they were on their way to America. It was almost hard to believe that it was true. You would hear them say, *"Es ist wahr!* [It is true!]" *"Wie kann es möglich sein!* [How can it be possible!]"

It did not take very long for each passenger to make a number of new friends, and soon, clusters of men and women would be seen here and there, each telling the other of his or her sorrows or good fortune. All in all it was a very jovial setting, and it seemed that the long journey across the Atlantic was to be a feast of happiness. Few noticed the whitecaps that were looming ahead. However, even some of the most high-spirited and laughing jokers suddenly felt the pit of their stomachs

Crowded on Deck During Voyage Across the Atlantic
From Lavern Rippley, **Auswanderung Bremen-USA,**
Bremerhave, West Germany, 1976.

rotating, and a kind of castor-oil taste come up into their mouths. People began taking leave without announcing their departure, and within an unbelievably short time, not a person was seen on deck. Where had they all gone to? Were they having a friendly party somewhere below deck? I did not want to lose out on the fun, so I began to hunt for them. Then, suddenly, I too felt some kind of uneasiness, and before I got very far, it was on me. I was a seasick man. After the seasickness took hold of the passengers, the friendly gatherings on deck were over, and all joviality on that voyage across the Atlantic came to an end. The only word I can find to describe the feeling is one word: "rotten."

We first sighted land on this side of the Atlantic on May 14, an event I shall never forget. I know that I was wondering just what the land would look like at close quarters. I had heard so much about the wild, wide, unsettled country that had open arms of welcome to all comers. I expected to see large, flat, treeless prairies with no one living on them — except for droves of Indians here and there, flocks of wild game, and wild herds of antelope, deer, and buffalo ranging on the plains. I was

Eureka, Dakota Territory in 1896
From **Harper's Weekly**, *July 11, 1896.*

I was

very much surprised when we came near enough to land to see large towns, smoking chimneys, and skyscrapers. I could not understand how this could be the land of the homesteader. Even Bremen in Germany was no match for this giant, New York City. But I was told that it was different far inland, so I expected to see the large empty spaces some hours after getting out of New York City. But after a day and night by fast train, the situation had not changed; we were running into large cities all the time, one larger than the other, and this kept up a considerable time after we had entered Dakota Territory. Before lying down to sleep the fifth night on the fast train, I said to a friend, *"Ich gehe zu Bett. Wachen Sie mir morgen früh.* [I'm going to bed. Wake me tomorrow morning.]" But before I got to sleep, the trainmen came through the car shouting, "Eureka! Eureka! The next station is Eureka!" It had been dark for several hours, and we had not been able to see how the country looked. We were afraid that we would not be able to find our way from the station to Hague, the place we wanted to go. We thought that Eureka also was one of those large cities that we had seen so many of since we started from New York.

When the train stopped, the train people came and got us off and led us into the depot where they saw to it that we got all our bundles of clothing. As I set down the last bundle, a man from behind said to me,

"Ich freue mich Sie zu sehen [I am glad to see you]." It was an old friend of mine that had come with a team from Hague to meet me and our party and take us to the settlement where many people from our home in Russia had homesteaded. Believe me, I was glad to see that man. It was Philip Gross, a relative of my wife, whom we had not seen for many years. But we knew him instantly. He told us to get ready to start for the 40-mile trip to the Hague country.

But I said, "Can you find your way when it is so dark?"

"Yes," he replied, "I have made this trip many a time when it was darker than it is now."

We started out, and it took hours and hours before the dawn of day commenced to break. I remarked several times that it seemed to be very cold in this part of the country, but Philip paid slight attention. When it became light enough, I saw large drifts of snow lying all over the country. "My garsh!" I thought, "Is this the North Pole?" When we left Russia the weather was warm, no snow was left on the ground, and the farmers were almost finished with the spring's work. Here it was almost full winter yet. I asked Mr. Gross how long this snow would be around, and he replied that it would all be gone in a few days, as it would soon be the first of April, and the snow very seldom stayed on any longer than that. By this time it had become light enough so that I could see far out in every direction, and what a sight it was: not a house to be seen for miles and miles. Now and then we could see the smoke coming up from some settler's sod house. Those settlers were miles apart. Yes, now we had reached the large territory that was open to new settlers, and my fear of being disappointed in getting a homestead of my own had vanished for good.

It was almost noon by the time we reached the Hague settlement, and was I glad when Mr. Gross pointed to a small object at the side of a large hill situated about five miles away and told us that it was his home and that his wife would have a good dinner ready.

After we finished dinner, we went to bed and slept until evening. I was so very tired from the long trip. The next day Mr. and Mrs. Gross hitched up their team and took me to see many German friends that had left Russia previously and had already found land settled on their homesteads. All of those people were glad to talk to me and to hear the latest news from their former homes, and all of them were anxious to get me located on a homestead. This was not so easily done as one would think because most of the homestead land around Hague was already taken or filed on. Many places were subject to "jumping" because the homesteader had not lived on the land or done the required improvement, but it was thought best not to trouble anyone since there was much land available for homesteads farther out. However, there remained a quarter section close in that had not been filed on, and I was advised to take it, so I did.

But after staying on that place for seven years and finding no water, I gave it up. It was too hard to haul water for the house and the stock winter and summer. The nearest I could get water was three miles away, and in the winter, many days, the cattle had to go without water. After farming — or,

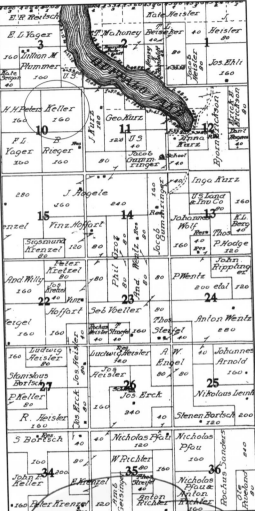

West Side of Alaxanter Township
Max Keller's homestead in Section 10 near Buffalo Lake is circled. The predominance of German names indicate the number of Keller's neighbors who joined him in the rush to Pierce County in 1906.
From the **Standard Atlas of Pierce County, North Dakota**, compiled and published by Geo. A. Ogle & Co., Chicago, 1910.

rather, trying to farm — on that land for seven years and hardly raising a single good crop, I found it necessary to go to other parts of the country to look for work. My neighbor, Anton Wentz, had gone into the Buffalo Lake country in North Dakota, and there he saw a large district of homestead land that had plenty of water on it. One could claim many quarters of land that had fresh water springs or lakes on them. When he returned with that good news, a large number of us made a rush for that part of the country and settled there. Most of us had proved up our first homesteads within the eighteen months and paid $1.25 per acre, and in that way we could take a new homestead — but we would have to live on the new one five years before proving up.

When I came to North Dakota, it was still a territory, but it became a state before I moved from the Hague country. When I came to the Buffalo Lake country, situated in the western part of Pierce County, to look for another homestead, the main thing I wanted was water — and plenty of it. So I filed on a quarter that had a nice lake, a little creek, and several springs. I was told by others that this quarter contained a lot of waste land, but I wanted water and didn't care if half of it was waste if only I could have plenty of water for my cattle and household.

When I moved from Hague to the land that I homesteaded west of Esmond, I came in a covered wagon. I brought my family, two cows, a few young stock, three horses, a plow, a drag, a seeder, a few other implements, and my household goods. I built a sod house the first summer, as well as a stable for the horses and cattle. The nearest town was Harvey, about 20 miles away. I did not experience any hardships after coming here, but while I was in the Hague country, my family suffered many times from a lack of plentiful food, and we had to go without proper clothing part of time. But we did not complain because over in Russia we had to take that often.

My father remained on the Hague homestead until he died.

Teaching in Russia, Farming in McHenry County: The Saga of a *Wolhyniendeutsche* Couple

The Adolf Klebes

If we had known all we would have to do in North Dakota, we would have stayed in Germany, or at least New York.

The Klebe family migrated from Brandenberg, Prussia to Polish Russia, Volhynia, in the early 1800s, settling in the village of Blumenthal to the west of Kiev. Adolf was born to Frederich and Anna Biberdorf Klebe in 1861. Adolf's father was a successful farmer who, to use the son's words, was "comfortably well off." So were Adolf and his wife, Henrietta; she had a maid to help with the children and a woman to do the wash. In spite of this, Russification policies drove them out of Volhynia to North Dakota.

Street in Sadki, Volhynia
Adolf Klebe came from a well-wooded region where houses were built of wood. The streets of the villages were often as wide as 200 yards so fruit and vegetable gardens could be grown in the center.
From Dr. Karl Stumpp, **The German-Russians**, *translated by Joseph S. Height (Lincoln, Nebraska: Reprint by the American Historical Society of Germans from Russia, 1978).*

WENT TO A COLONY SCHOOL with one teacher in charge. There were many children in the room; long tables lined the sides of the room, one for the girls on one side and one for the boys on the other. We used quill pens. I went to this school until I was about fifteen, one year after I was confirmed. Then I went to a seminary for a few years in preparation for teaching and the ministry. I was not ordained as a minister of the Gospel, but I could baptize, preach, and bury the dead.

I started teaching when I was twenty-one in 1882 and taught until 1895. I had learned how to farm, to weave, and many industrial kinds of work, but I did not use that knowledge in Russia.

At first, I taught only in the German language, but gradually the period for teaching Russian was lengthened, until at last, I had to teach it almost entirely and could give German only one hour a day. I was also expected to direct the school choir.

Life became rather complex there. Toward the last, there was so much politics that one had to change one's religion to have a good position. I never had to apply for a position as teachers do in America: I went where I was sent. I was offered a good position on the condition that I become a member of the Greek Catholic Church. Since I, a Lutheran, did not agree with the doctrines of this church, I decided to emigrate to America.

I married Henrietta Wolter on June 19, 1883, at Heimthal, Russia. We had five children born in Russia; one of them died in infancy. The others we brought to America.

We left Russia the last part of April in 1895. Being a teacher, I made the most of the trip. I had lived in comfortable circumstances in the old country and took advantage of the journey to see the most important places en route. It was a wonderful trip. I had enough curiosity about things to poke around and find out all I could on the way. We visited Hemel, Thorns, Berlin, and Hamburg en route to the ship. We were thirteen days on board ship, the *Prussia*.

We stopped in New York City and visited many places of interest. We stopped in Buffalo, Cleveland, and Detroit on the way to Duluth where I saw the bridge open across the lake to let ships go under it. Then we went to St. Paul and from there to Cando. If we had known all we would have to do in North Dakota, we would have stayed in Germany, or at least in New York. I had no idea that wheat would sell as cheaply as 30 cents a bushel nor that farming was such hard work.

I filed on land near Willow City in 1896. For a while we lived in a sod house until we could get a place built for ourselves. This place belonged to a neighbor and was close to the Mouse River. There was a settlement of Icelanders on the Mouse and from there on, nothing. I pulled out logs for my own house and built it in 1897 with the help of neighbors.

The house had only one room, divided in the center by the fireplace and with curtains. We had a dugout for a root cellar. The house had a stone foundation, and at first we whitewashed it. When the rain washed off the whitewash and the chinking fell out, we put tin around the outside.

I built a sod barn, about 16 by 22 feet, on the claim, which was seven miles from where we were living. I also plowed 28 acres of land with my ponies and seeded it to wheat. While I was dong this, Reinhold Klebe and Rudolf Biberdorf, relatives of mine, were working on their places near me. All of them lived during the week in a little house, five by six feet. They had a stove inside, but no floor. They took in a board at night, one at a time, put a sack of hay on it, and lay down to sleep. Only one could get in at a time, for it took maneuvering to get the board in through the small place, and the last one in had to close the door.

Although I prospered at farming, I did not like working from 4:00 in the morning until 11:30 at night. I followed the threshing machine for four falls and worked hard to make a living.

We had three horses and two cows. The first crop was the 28 acres of wheat that I planted. I was able to plow only a few inches deep with my three ponies, and on July 4th, we could not see any wheat. In 1900 we had 400 bushes of good wheat and 700 bushels of market grade; others had very little. In 1901 and 1902 we had good crops. In 1903 we bought another farm — a quarter-section and 40 acres.

I always wanted to get away from North Dakota and made a couple of attempts to do so. In 1906 I went to Medicine Hat in the Cypress Hills of Canada to homestead, but someone had beaten me to it. They gave me back my filing fee. While I was in Canada, my wife hired a man to put in some flax. We got 400 bushels of flax that fall from the 20 acres. When I came home, unsuccessful in getting a new homestead, we decided to build a new eight-room house and a barn. By Christmas that year it was all paid for — the flax crop was the most important reason why.

We also thought of going to Lodi, California, but in 1909, I got word from my daughter, Lydia, not to come because she was ill. Both Lydia and her husband died of trichinosis. Their child, Johanna, was ill, but she recovered. We took her in and brought our granddaughter up as our own. Clara, another daughter, was also ill, but she recovered. We went to California for six months, but we did not stay.

About that time I began hiring a man to do the farming for me, and I did the managing. I liked to go fishing, and I believe that there probably is not a settler along the Mouse River who has caught more fish than I have.

what is FLAX

Working the Land and Working for God

The Gottfried Kurtz Family

Mother very often walked to Carrington, a distance of 15 miles.

Daniel Kurtz's grandparents migrated from Germany to Warsaw after eastern Poland fell under Russian control. His father, Gottfried, and his mother, Christina, were born there in the 1840s. After they married, they moved to Kiev where Daniel was born in 1877. Gottfried farmed on a small scale, but he earned his living as a wheelwright. Increasingly upset over the way Russia was treating its Germans, in 1877 Gottfried decided to take his family to the United States. Daniel was ten years old at the time. He tells the family's story.

*T*HROUGH CORRESPONDENCE WITH FRIENDS in America, my father learned that this country was a land of opportunities and a free country, where a person was at liberty to do as he liked: free schools, free religion, free government lands for anyone of legal age. When he learned all this, he decided to emigrate, the sooner the better.

So, in September 1887, he sold all his personal belongings, except bedding and clothing, said farewell to his relatives and friends, and purchased passage for himself and my mother; his two sons, me and Christian; and a young man who was a distant relative.

The steamship we came on was an old boat, slow and cumbersome, and it took us 19 days to cross the ocean. We landed in New York the first part of October 1887. From there to Carrington, Dakota Territory, our destination, took three more days, a total trip of 22 days.

Immediately upon our arrival at Carrington, father went in search of government land. He located and pre-empted on the NW¼ of Section 4, Township 147, Range 68, Wells County. After filing at Sykeston, he made preparations to build a temporary home in which to live during the winter. While building, we resided with John Piedt, who lived nearby. Father excavated a hole 14- by 28-feet, two-feet deep. The rest of the walls were built of sod laid in brick-like fashion until he had a six-foot high wall on one side and one eight feet high on the other, so as to make a slant roof. The end wall was also of sod. The roof boards, stringers, windows, and doors were of lumber purchased and hauled with ox team and wagon from Carrington, a distance of 15 miles.

The house was divided into two compartments, one where we lived, ate, and slept; the other for the stock — two oxen and a cow. The building had only two windows, one in each room, and three doors, one leading out from the residence part, one in the partition, and one in the stable. The floor in both parts was of the solid earth.

Father built all of the furniture — his experience with carpenter's tools came in well. The bedstead, chairs, benches, and cupboard were neatly and well made and painted. The cook stove was a small cast-iron four-hole one. For heating, we followed the Russian style by building a furnace, a fireplace affair of homemade clay bricks. It was seven feet long, six feet high, and 30 inches deep with horizontal partitions about a foot apart with a hole in one end of the bottom partition; the next had a hole or opening in the opposite end, and so on. This caused the heat and hot smoke to zig-zag through the furnace before it reached the chimney.

We used for fuel hay twisted into hard rolls or prairie (buffalo) chips. We would fire in the morning until it was thoroughly heated, and this heat would hold all day, keeping the room comfortable. In the evening we would repeat the firing, and this would keep our home warm until morning.

Mother very often walked to Carrington, a distance of 15 miles, carrying the butter and eggs which she traded for groceries. Sometimes she made the trip in one day; other times she would stay overnight with friends, returning the next day. Later they did their trading at Sykeston, only about ten miles away.

In the fall of 1892, when the Soo Railroad was built as far as Cathay, that town became our trading point. It was about four miles away. Up until the fall of 1892, we hauled all the grain raised on the farm to Carrington or Sykeston, where we also purchased all the commodities needed for the home.

Mother made, by hand, all our clothing. She made her dresses of calico and gingham goods and underwear from fleece-lined cotton goods. The men's clothing she made of blue denim for outerwear and fleece-lined goods for underwear. I got my first ready-made suit when I was 15 years of age.

Father had great difficulty in finding water on the claim. He dug and drilled in six different places to depths between 20 and 208 feet.

Digging a Well in Dakota
From the Fred Hultstrand History in Pictures Collection, NDIRS-NDSU, Fargo, N.D.

The fifth well he dug by hand to 108 feet, then bored with a test auger 100 feet deeper, making a total depth of 208 feet. There was no sign of water.

However, in the summer of 1902, he located water a half a mile from where the buildings stood. He struck a plentiful supply of water in gravel. This well held out as long as father resided on the homestead. Up to 1902, we had to haul most of our water from Cathay.

Father made a final proof on his pre-emption in the fall of 1888, and that same year he homesteaded on the NE¼ of Section 8, Township 147, Range 68, Wells County. But he did not move onto it until 1890, when he erected a frame house where he lived until he retired from farming.

As father had to do his grain marketing and trading at Sykeston, a distance of 10 miles, or Carrington, a distance of 15 miles, in the early years, he always tried to haul his fuel and other supplies the same time he sold grain in the fall of the year before winter set in. He only had oxen to drive. This could not always be done, because sometimes he could not get his grain threshed until very late in the fall. In 1890 he did not get his grain threshed early enough to get it to market before winter set in. He barely had time to buy his winter's supplies. So, as soon as the weather moderated in the spring of 1891, he tried to get some wheat to market. As he did not own a granary, he had wheat in a pile in the yard, covered with straw and some boards on top of the straw to hold it down. In the evening of March 7, 1891, father and I had loaded wheat onto the wagon so we could take it to Sykeston the following morning. The weather in the afternoon and evening of the 7th was mild but kind of hazy. Toward the morning of the 8th, a blizzard struck. It lasted all day. When, after the storm, we went to see about the load of wheat, we found every kernel had been blown out of the box, a box which held 60 bushels.

The first crop in 1888 was 70 bushels of wheat. A heavy frost that year cut the yield and quality. What we did get we used for seed. One day that summer of 1888 my father was working for his neighbor, Charley Smith. Mr. Smith had a well on his farm that was curbed with rocks. This well was to be cleaned, so he wanted father to go down into the well and shovel the debris into a bucket which Mr. Smith would pull up on a windlass. Father took one look into the well. That was enough; he shook his head and refused to go down. He tried to tell Mr. Smith in very broken English that it was too dangerous, that some of the rocks were loose and might fall to the bottom and kill whoever might be working down there. Father did not go down. While Mr. Smith and father were arguing, a bachelor who lived nearby came to the place. Mr. Smith told him that he had a hired man, my father, who refused to do his bidding, that he was afraid to go down into the well. The bachelor said he was not afraid; he went down. He had cleaned it all. Mr. Smith was pulling up the last bucket when it touched a loose rock, which fell and hit the bachelor on the head and killed him. Father was that close to death.

I remained at home with my parents and worked on the farm until I was 26 years old, except for the time I attended school. At the age of eight, I was enrolled in a parochial school where, besides religion, I was taught some reading, writing, spelling, and arithmetic. When I was eleven, I started attending a rural district public school. I went there in Woodward School District, Wells County, until I finished the third reader and the other subjects that went with it — the same as finishing third grade.

During the winter of 1893-94 I received instruction from our Baptist pastor, where I stayed throughout the winter. From then on I attended the rural school about four months each winter until I was 26 years old. Then I went to Lincoln, Nebraska, where I took up the study for the Adventist ministry, a course I finished except for one year of Greek and one of Hebrew. The rest of my education was in the school of hard knocks.

I followed the ministry for six years, when I retired because of ill health on the advice of my doctor, who suggested that I settle on a farm. I did so in 1911 on Section 9, Sykeston Township in Wells County. I remained there for 23 years.

In 1901, while I was attending a Bible school at Columbus, South Dakota, I met and became acquainted with Miss Margaret Wall, who was preparing for missionary work. We were united in marriage, and to our happy union, three children were born.

Farming With Oxen

Above, Family in Front of Sod House with Oxen & Horses
Below, Heading for the Hay Field with Team of Oxen

*Photographs from
the Fred
Hultstrand History
in Pictures
Collection
NDIRS-NDSU,
Fargo, N.D.*

From Germany to Russia, to Turkey, to Rumania (without moving), to Canada, to America: *Dobrudschadeutsche*

The George and August Leitner Families

Even the beard on a man's face was taxed. . . .

George Leitner was born in Rorbach, Germany in 1822. When his devoutly Roman Catholic parents insisted that he become a priest, he migrated to southern Russia on the Black Sea in 1839. He worked as a farm laborer. He lost his first wife and their baby in childbirth but married again to Elizabeth. They had four children while they resided in southern Russia. Because land was scarce in the early 1860s, the Leitners emigrated along with many German-Russian to the Dobrudja region of northern Turkey on the western shore of the Black Sea. George found a fertile piece of land, and the Turks left the new colonists alone. Four more children were born into the family. After Russia defeated Turkey in an 1877 war, the Dobrudja region became part of Rumania; the Rumanians imposed very heavy taxes on the Germans from Russia, and many, including the Leitners, left for America. August Leitner, the youngest child who was born in Turkey in 1875, tells his father's story as well as his own.

A SHORT WHILE BEFORE THE RUSSO-TURKISH WAR, a Russian spy built a house in the village in which we lived. When laying the roof tiles, which were of various colors, he laid them in such a way that it made a code which could be seen by the Russian officers and soldiers that camped across the river in Russian territory through spy glasses. This code told the Russians about all activities of the Turks. As the spy could not seem to get the tiles laid right, but had to relay them time and time again, the Turks became suspicious and finally were convinced that he was a spy sending messages.

They picked him off with a rifle, but it was too late. Cossacks swam with their horses across the river on a dark night and attacked the village. They slaughtered men, women, and children. The Cossacks took and carried away everything they could find. Children were stabbed and tossed from soldier to soldier with spears; women were disemboweled and men butchered. Our family was able to hide from the Cossacks, but we lost all of our property.

Then we came under new rulers (Rumanians), and taxes became unbearable. They taxed everything a person owned. For instance, each window pane was taxed a certain amount; they levied taxes on each person and their possessions and property. Even the beard on a man's face was taxed. At that time, all men wore full beards with great pride, but when the beard was taxed, all the men shaved them off.

Under the Rumanians the people could not make enough to pay the taxes and have enough left to live off. So our family and sixteen other families decided to get out of the country.

Two friends of my father, Sam Piedt and a Mr. Wentland, had emigrated to America in 1882, and my father had been corresponding with these men. They spoke so well of America that father decided to emigrate there. So, in the spring of 1885, our family and sixteen others bought passage to Carrington, Dakota Territory, and left Rumania for America.

However, when father and the families arrived at New York, they were met by fast-talking Canadian agents who talked them into changing their course and going to Canada. The changed transportation tickets took them to Capel, Manitoba, Canada.

When they arrived there, all the families were penniless, so they had to stay. Otherwise, the seventeen families would have left for Carrington immediately. In the fall of 1885, father moved into Winnipeg where father worked at common labor until the spring of 1887. By then, he saved enough money to take the family to Carrington, but all they had was our clothing.

We settled on a pre-emption in Foster County about five miles south of Carrington, where other Rumanian Germans had settled. That summer, father traveled around some, looking for a better location than we had. He found it in Wells County, land he liked much better. He left his pre-emption and homesteaded on the NW¼ of Section 18, Township 148, Range 68.

As soon as he filed his homestead, he built our first real home in America, a house made of a mixture of clay and straw with a shingled pitched roof. We used the attic as a bedroom. The house measured 14 by 28 feet, partitioned inside with the same material used on the walls. One room served as living room, dining room. and kitchen. The other was the bedroom. There were three windows, one for the bedroom and two for the other room; and two doors, one for the exit and one in the partition. We got what lumber we needed in Carrington, where we also bought what furniture we needed. We used kerosene lamps for light, a cast-iron stove for cooking, and a hot-blast heater where we burned prairie chips and hay.

The church played an important part in our lives. While in Russia, we were part of the German Baptist community. After we immigrated to Turkey, we joined another German Baptist Church, which father served as a deacon.

There was a small German Baptist congregation five miles south of Carrington which was organized in 1884. It served Foster and Wells counties. In 1884 and 1885, a number of German Baptists settled in what would become Germantown, Woodward, and Fairville townships in Wells County. A layman, Fred Edinger, was appointed to conduct services — the first was held in his home on March 8, 1886. After we moved into the area, some services were held in our home.

The Germantown Baptist Church
"Gott ist Liebe — God is Love" is written
beneath the steeple of what became known as
"The Church by the Highway."
From Fessenden: A Centennial History, 1893-1993,
published by the Fessenden Centennial Committee, 1993.

Reverend A.F. Brauns came from south of Carrington to hold services once every two weeks for almost two years. He was paid from offerings taken at each service and also received some compensation from the Mission Society.

Immediately upon settling his claim, father joined the congregation and became active. In 1887, Reverend William Achterberg was called to serve this station. He homesteaded as well in Germantown Township and served the congregation for three years.

The congregation met in private homes until 1888, when the school district built a schoolhouse, where services were held until 1893. The congregation began building a church in 1892 on a two-acre lot donated by Andrew Dietz. Christ Banik donated five acres for the cemetery. The lumber and other materials cost $1,500, which we met with subscription. All labor was donated; Reverend John Jaeger, who was a carpenter by trade, acted as foreman.

Just after the building was up and shingling started, a cyclonic wind struck and flattened the whole structure to the ground. Nineteen men were working at the time, but they saw the storm and were able to get away, so no one was hurt.

This was a severe blow to the congregation, but members started all over in the spring of 1893 and finished the church in June, when it was dedicated.

In 1898, father died, and we buried him in the church cemetery.

My story begins in Turkey, where I was born. I had to work beginning when I was six years old. We cut the grain with a scythe and bound it by hand with bands of straw, made in large number by the men. We children had to carry these bands to men as they needed them. We also had to pick up loose straws of grain and gather them into piles.

When I reached eight years, I attended the village school where I was taught in both the Rumanian and German languages for six months each winter.

I came to America with my family in 1885 when I was nine and one-half years old. I did not stay in Canada with my parents. I went with my sister Mary and her husband John Piedt to Melville. When we arrived there, we all walked five miles to Sam Piedt's home where we stayed until John Piedt established a home on a claim.

I lived with my sister for three years and did not move back with father and the rest of the family until they were settled in Wells County. I worked as a laborer in the community until I was eighteen years of age. Then I bought a quarter of land on crop payment contract valued at $1,300. In the spring of 1894, John V. Zuber wanted to buy the quarter and offered me $1,800 for it. A $500 profit in so short a time I thought too good a thing to pass up, so I sold the quarter to Mr. Zuber.

I was foot-loose again. I worked again as a farm laborer in the community until 1897 when I homesteaded on a claim in the area of Anamoose in McHenry County. That year I built a small homestead shack and batched while I broke 40 acres. After fourteen months, I commuted and sold it.

Then I came back to Wells County and bought a quarter of land in Oshkosh Township from my brother Fred. He had broken 40 acres and built an L-shaped house of lumber. One part was 14 by 16 feet, the other 14 by 18 — one story, with an attic. He also built a small barn and dug a shallow well. He built a new house in 1910. Before that, I lived with him.

In 1897 I had met Miss Barbara Sauter whose parents had migrated from southern Russia. We married in 1902 and had seven children: Otto, Marie,George, Paul, Fred, Ella, and Theodore. With a growing family, we moved out of my brother's house and built a large two-story house in 1910.

August and Barbara Leitner, Married in 1902
From **Fessenden: A Centennial History, 1893-1993**, *published by the Fessenden Centennial Committee, 1993.*

The Depot in Fessenden, Wells County
From **Fessenden: A Centennial History, 1893-1993**,
published by the Fessenden Centennial Committee, 1993.

Not All Homestead Life was Drab and Humorless

The Christian Maiers

This team of one ox and one cow was just like crazy.

Christian Maier (born 1822) and Carolina Radi were third-generation Germans who settled in southern Russia. He farmed and was the village of Berresena's shoemaker. Their eldest son, Christian Jr., was born in 1862. He attended German school for eight years and worked on his father's farm into his early twenties. In 1884 he married Gottliebina Maier (no relation), and in 1886 they had the first of eleven children, Amelia, the only of their children born in Russia. That same year the Maiers left Russia because of overpopulation and land shortage.

SOME TIME AROUND 1884, my brother, Michael, journeyed to America and took up land in McIntosh County, Dakota Territory. Seeing that one could take up quite a bit of land in this country, Michael wrote to me and my parents telling us we should waste no time and come to the United States as soon as possible. As southern Russia was thickly populated and as the peasants did not have very much land on which to earn a living, we decided to prepare for a journey to America. This was my reason; I did not fear military service in the Russian army.

In the early part of April 1886, I, my wife, our daughter, Amelia, and my parents and younger brother, Frederic, decided to go. We traveled by wagon and a team of horses from Berresena to Leipzig (south Russia), 14 miles to the west. There we boarded a train bound for Bremen, Germany. We journeyed through Rumania and Austria to get there in two days. We had to wait in Bremen for eight days because there were no ships in port. But the delay didn't cost us anything as we had made our reservations and arrived just as a ship was leaving. The steamship company paid our living expenses until another ship came.

Boarding a steamer called *Vera*, we — accompanied by the Andrew Schadlers, Frederick Beglaus, Honus Beglaus, Johann Belders, Philip Reitlings, Gottlieb Bodemars, and Gottlieb Doblers — began our trip to America. The ship was in good condition, but the voyage was very rough because of storms. Most of the passengers were seasick. Many times while I lay flat on my back in my room I wished that I had remained in Russia. When the sea calmed, our outlook was better. The trip across the Atlantic to New York City took nine days.

Then we all traveled by train to Ellendale, Dakota. Settlers who had gone before us and established claims in McIntosh County came with horses, oxen, and wagons to pick us up. I had $20 when I arrived in Ellendale. Gottlieb Nitshke, my cousin who lived about six or seven miles southeast of what would become Ashley, came to get my family.

We stayed with the Nitshkes until we could file on land. Sometime in May 1886, I filed a pre-emption on a quarter in Antelope Township. My father gave me money so I could start paying for the claim. In June, my wife and I built a 12- by 18-foot sod house with a door and two windows. The walls, floor, and most of the roof were made from chunks of sod, lime, and clay. With some of my $20, I bought a little lumber to make the roof. With the rest, we bought food — enough, we hoped, to last until I could get more money.

At first, my parents and brother lived with us. Father purchased a wagon, two oxen, and a cow in Ellendale; and we traveled by oxen and wagon for a while. In 1886, one could still find buffalo bones nearly any place. I didn't have to travel very far to pick a wagon box full. One of the oxen was very lazy and slow of foot, but the cow was opposite in this respect. So after I gathered a load of buffalo bones, I hitched the cow and the other ox to the wagon. Along with other settlers, I started for Ellendale.

This team of one ox and one cow was just like crazy. They would run nearly all the time, and I had a hard time guiding them in the right direction. Ellendale was 35 miles cross-country from my home. I had gathered some of the bones 35 miles west and north of home because those close at hand soon disappeared. I could not hold my odd team in check, and I steadily drew away from the rest of the party. We had started early in the morning and had figured on camping out overnight and going into Ellendale the next day. When I got into the hilly country about 15 miles from my farm, my odd team, running most of the time, ran the wagon, filled with bones, into a trap of big rocks. Part of the load spilled as we went over the rocks. Then the team became stubborn and would not move for a while. Getting down on the front end of the wagon tongue, I scared the beasts enough so they bounded out over the rocks and took us out of the predicament. I stayed on the front end of tongue. When we got into Monango territory, the ox and cow ran into a creek

Settlers with the Cash Crop, *Buffalo Bones Gathered in the 1880s*
Photograph from **Eureka: 1887-1937**, *a publication of Eureka's Golden Jubilee Organization in 1937 which was edited by the Federal Writer's Project of the Works Progress Administration.*

that had a quite a bit of water. I let them rest a while before trying to get them started again. They would not move; the wagon was stuck in the creek.

An Englishman named Schimmelmore who was working in a field nearby came to my assistance. We unhitched the ox and cow and got them out of the creek. Then Mr. Schimmelmore hitched three of his horses to the wagon, now no longer quite so full of bones, and pulled it out. I hitched the cow and ox to the load again and sat down once more on the front of the wagon tongue. With the animals running once again, I reached Ellendale that same evening. I sold the bones for $4 a ton — and a ton was about all I had left. I stayed the night in Ellendale, purchased my supplies the next morning, and started for home. Again, the ox and cow ran most of the way. About ten miles out of Ellendale I met the party I started out with. They asked where I had been; they couldn't believe that I had already been to town until I showed them the supplies I purchased. My family was also surprised to see me so soon.

In 1887 my ten acres of flax yielded only 50 bushels, not much. With the crop conditions not very good, I decided to go farther east by myself and try to get a job in the harvest fields and on threshing rigs, which I did for $1.25 per day.

We planted an onion in a box in the house our first winter. We took good care of it, watering it at just the right time. When it was big enough and had grown stems, we took off the stems and ate them along with bread and the head of a pig which I could buy in Ellendale from time to time. We thought such a meal was a feast.

Sometime in 1887, my neighbor Andrew Schadler went to Ellendale. A widow lived alongside the trail to town, and she could not speak the German language; she was of English descent. She raised chickens and sold some at times. Andrew stopped there one day and bought two hens. He took them home — his first chickens. A short time afterwards, while on his way back from Ellendale, he stopped at the widow's farm again. He could not speak English, she could not speak German. He wanted to buy a rooster, but he couldn't make himself understood. Finally he said, in very broken English, "I want a chicken's man."

The woman replied, "Oh, so you are a poultry buyer and buy and sell chickens!"

Andrew did not know what to do to make her understand that he wanted to buy a rooster. Finally, seeing a high pile of waste in the yard, he climbed on top, clapped his hands, flapped his arms and crowed.

The lady exclaimed, "Oh, you want a rooster?"

"Yes, yes, rooster, rooster," said Andrew.

In 1888 I built my second home of the same material as the first. This one was 14 by 20 feet with two rooms, four windows, and a door. In 1893 I tore it down and built a third with lumber and shingles. It was the same size, but it had three rooms. I built my fourth and last home on the farm in 1895 in Antelope Township of lumber, cement, plaster, and shingles. It was two stories, 24 by 28 feet. I also built a good barn and dug a deep well. I spent $3,000 on my last home.

Chicken Coop, Early Dakota Style
From the Fred Hultstrand History in Pictures Collection, NDIRS-NDSU, Fargo, N.D.

A Colony in Search of a Better Life

The Johann Millers

Very often the soup would be full of ashes.

Johann Miller was born to August and Wilhelmina Miller on December 30, 1857, in Kulm of the Bessarabia region of southern Russia. He attended German-language schools and helped with farm work. At age 19 he married Wilhelmina Miller in February 1877. He and his wife farmed with his parents and raised four of their own children. In 1885 the lure of free land in a free country brought them to the United States. Like so many of their fellow Germans from Russia, the Millers became a part of a colony of homestead seekers who settled in close proximity to one another.

M y BROTHER-IN-LAW, DANIEL GROSZ, had sailed for America in 1878 and had taken up land in the vicinity of Parkston, Dakota Territory. He wrote urging us to come to the United States. In his letters he stated that there was plenty of land in Dakota Territory and that the chances to make a better livelihood were far better than in south Russia. He told us that one could take up land for practically nothing and that free speech, free religion and a free country to live in made it a pleasure to reside in the United States.

On November 6, 1885, I, my wife, and our three sons — Gottfried, Johann and Gustave — and our daughter, Mathilda, left Gnadenfelt in south Russia in a wagon drawn by a team of horses and traveled to

Kowshan, south Russia. Here we boarded a train bound for Bremen, Germany. It took three days to reach this German seaport.

On the morning after arriving on November 9, we were fortunate to find a steamer in port waiting for passengers bound for America. We got on board the ship bound for New York City. The meals and beds on the ship were good, but we had no appetite because we were seasick.

We reached the shores of America, New York City, on November 18, 1885. We boarded a train bound for Scotland, Dakota. The trip took three days. We had to remain in Scotland for one day before someone came to get us. August Stelzer, a farmer living 22 miles northwest of Scotland, whose wife was my wife's cousin, came with a team of horses and a wagon to get our family. It took four hours to travel the 22 miles to the Stelzer's farm, where we stayed overnight. The next morning Mr. Stelzer took us to the Daniel Grosz farm, located about five miles north of the Stelzer place.

The cost of the trip from Kowshan in south Russia to Scotland, Dakota Territory was one hundred and sixteen Russian rubles (about $58). I still had money left to purchase stock when the time arrived for us to travel north from the Grosz farm.

We lived with my brother-in-law during the winter of 1885-86 and spring of 1886. He did not charge any board or room for us, but I and my wife helped with the farm work and did all we could to earn our keep.

At that point we were joined by seven other families to form a colony group to take up land in Springfield Township, McIntosh County, Dakota. We were joined by the Johann Krolls, the August Millers, the Gottlieb Schneiders, the Carl Hilliuses, the Daniel Roloffs, my brother-in-law's family the Daniel Groszes, and the Ludvig Billigmeirs. On the 3rd of May, 1886, after I had purchased two cows for $45, a team of horses for $225, and two oxen for $120, the colony group built their wagons into covered wagons. The men had iron frames made in the blacksmith shop in Parkston and fastened them to the wagons. With flax sacks and other cloth, which we had brought over from Russia, we made rough-looking covered wagons for the trip into the northern part of Dakota Territory.

When I left the Parkston territory with these colonists. I changed off using the horses and the oxen. The older children drove the livestock. They walked all the way to the railroad point, a distance of 25 miles north of Parkston.

While at Mitchell I and my father August, who joined us after my mother died, loaded a boxcar with our livestock, feed, and personal belongings for the rail trip to Ellendale. On the 7th of May we unloaded our wagons, livestock, feed, clothing, bedding and personal belongings and started to begin the homestead search. Our eight families arrived at Hoskins on the 9th of May. John Wishek was the land-office agent representing the United States government. Our colony group remained in Hoskins for four days looking for suitable locations to take up homesteads and pre-emption claims.

On May 13, 1886, I filed on a homestead on the SW¼ of Section 34, Township 132 and Range 67 in Springfield Township, McIntosh County. On May 15 our family moved onto the land. During the first week we lived under our wagon box. After a space the size of the wagon box and four-feet deep was dug, the end gate of the wagon was taken out and the vehicle was tipped upside down over the dugout space. Because the space was too small, the "hole in the ground" was made longer and wider. To keep the wagon box from falling into the hole, we put sod chunks into the end and sides on the four corners. This made more room for the family. The mosquitoes were very bad, so at night we gathered dry brush and weeds, which burned for a long time. We put them beside the wagon-box home and burned them as a smudge. Our sons slept side by side on one end of this home; and my wife, daughter, and I occupied the other end of this crude home. For cooking, we built a stove into a nearby hill by digging a hole and then a small one at the back to serve as a chimney. We cleaned out the dugout stove and cemented the walls and ceiling with lime. We gathered prairie brush and twisted hay for fuel. We found a large rock to cover the entrance. The stove got hot enough to bake bread and cook meat and vegetables. At times when soup was being cooked, the opening could not be closed. When a high wind came along and there were ashes in the opening, very often the soup would be full of ashes.

We began our first Dakota home, made of sod and lumber, on May 22, 1886. We made the walls of sod chunks, as well as most of the ceiling. We spent a few dollars for lumber at Ellendale to make a framework for

Community Gathers to Build Sod House
From the Fred Hultstrand History in Pictures Collection, NDIRS-NDSU, Fargo, N.D.

the roof. We pressed sod chunks in between these pieces of lumber on the roof to make it compact. Our sod shanty was 16 by 24 feet; it had two rooms, two doors, and four half-windows. We used kerosene for lighting. I went to the nearby lakes and sloughs and searched for smooth stones to make a heating and cooking combination stove. I used lime to construct the stove five feet long, two- and one-half feet wide, and about five feet high. In the winter of 1886-87 we stuffed it full of twisted hay and closed the opening so no heat would escape. The sod house was warm all night. We had to do the same thing every morning and evening.

In May 1887, we added a 14- by 16-foot addition of lumber to our home.

The first church services were conducted in Springfield on May 26, 1886, on our farm. Since our house was not big enough to hold all the people, I built on a lean-to from a wagon which I moved close to the sod house. It was just a framework covered with sacks of anything I could find to make shade. I made some benches out of boxes and pieces of lumber and put them under the lean-to. We did not have a minister, so Gottlieb Schneider read the scripture. Later we conducted services in other homes. In 1896 a church went up six miles west and seven miles south of the village of Kulm.

Our family gathered buffalo bones during the summer of 1886, sometimes with a team of oxen, others with a team of horses. We nailed

Heading Back to the Field for Another Load
From the Fred Hultstrand History in Pictures Collection, NDIRS-NDSU, Fargo, N.D.

wide boards to the sides and ends of the wagon box so that a bigger load could be gathered. I took the bones to Ellendale where I received from $8 to $10 a load.

My first crop in 1887 was barley and wheat. I used my two oxen and two horses, a hand plow, drag, and binder. I seeded the grain by hand and went over it with the drag afterwards — a total of two acres of barley and eight of wheat from which I harvested 25 bushels of barley and 100 bushels of wheat.

In the spring of 1892 I built another house where the first home stood, a two-story building constructed of lumber, plaster, cement and shingles. Six more children were born on the farm: Marie, Nathaniel, Lydia, Selma, Martha, and Paul. In 1910 I retired from farming, moved to Kulm, and practiced the carpentry trade.

Finding Prosperity on a Plains Homestead

Philip and Eva Mosbrucker

Those early years in Russia were not very good. — **Philip**

What a struggle my parents had in making a living in Russia. — **Eva**

Philip & Eva Mosbrucker
Photographed with eight of their children.
Oliver County: 1885-1985,
a publication of the Oliver County Historical Society, 1985.

Philip was born in 1864 to Peter and Eva Mosbrucker; Eva was born in 1866 to Joseph and Dorothy Meyer. Both families farmed on small tracts of land not very far from each other in southern Russia. They both attended common school, were confirmed in the Catholic religion, and worked hard on their families' farms. On October 15, 1886, the two childhood friends married and had two children by the time they emigrated to America. They had another ten after they homesteaded in Oliver County. Philip and Eva tell their stories individually.

Philip Mosbrucker's Story:

HOSE EARLY YEARS IN RUSSIA were not very good. Times were hard, income small because we all farmed small tracts of land — 30 or 40 acres — and no one had more than one team of horses, two cows, and a few chickens.

My father had some friends who had moved to Dakota Territory in 1883 and located in Mandan. They advised him to sell out his property in Russia and come to Dakota where homestead land was still open for filing at the cost of $14 and that building material was cheap as well — homes were made of sod and clay-mud and there was plenty of free coal for the digging. So father sold his property in the fall of 1888 and made arrangements to move to America shortly after Christmas.

I married Miss Eva Meyer on October 15, 1886. We made our home with my father — my mother had died in 1875. With some $400 from the proceeds of the sale, we bought third-class tickets and went on board the ship named *Mostom* on December 27, 1888. The ship had been in service for many years and was not considered safe to travel on in bad windstorms.

My wife, two children, my father, and I had come by train from Odessa, Russia, to Rotterdam to board ship for America. I will never forget how close we came to sinking. Six days out, a terrible storm rose. It lasted for three days and nights. Everybody on board knelt in prayer, asking that the storm subside. On the morning of the fourth day it quieted down, and we proceeded on our journey. The accommodations on the boat were not so good. The food was not fit to eat, and the sleeping quarters were not very clean. We furnished our own blankets and sacks filled with straw for mattresses. We also brought along a lot of good food that my wife prepared back in Russia.

After two or three days in New York, we boarded a train for Mandan where we were met by Joe Boehm and Martin Bartz, the friends of my father who had invited us to come.

Mandan, North Dakota in the Early Years
Photograph from the collection of the State Historical Society of North Dakota.

We lived in Mandan until the following spring when we moved out on the homestead I had selected and filed on in Oliver County. We did not have any money to speak of, but we did manage to build a small shack to live in a while. I had a neighbor break ten acres on the homestead which I seeded to flax, harvested, and realized a profit of $110. My labor on different jobs during the first summer brought in another $450. We continued to live in Mandan where I got steady employment during the winter and part of the summer months when I was not working on the farm. After proving up on the homestead, we decided to live in Mandan where there were good schools. I made a good income doing odd jobs around town every year, and after twelve years, I had saved some money. I decided to move out onto the homestead and make my living farming more land and raising livestock. While we were in Mandan, I had made improvements on the homestead every year. I was also able to buy adjoining land and increase our holding to 350 acres. With the help of my wife and children, we prospered and put money in the bank every year.

Eva (Meyer) Mosbrucker's Story:

WAS BORN IN KATERENA, RUSSIA, March 6, 1886. When I was seven years old, I started attending common school and continued until I was 14 and confirmed in the Catholic religion. During those years, I lived with my parents on the farm.

What a struggle my parents had in making a living in Russia! Our income was small. They would put in only about 20 acres of crop every year, and we milked three cows, which gave us barely enough milk and cream for our own use. We raised a large garden and sold a lot of the produce in a town two miles away. This was our only income in the summer months.

We made all our own clothing by spinning the wool into yarn and spending evenings knitting. Our buildings of stone and mud were not very healthy. Our house was always damp from frost, and ventilation

Germans-in-Russia Family Gather to Husk Corn
From Dr. Karl Stumpp, **The German-Russians**, *translated by Joseph S. Height*
(Lincoln, Nebraska: Reprint by the
American Historical Society of Germans from Russia, 1978).

Germans-in-Russia Women
Cook in a Summer Kitchen
From Dr. Karl Stumpp,
The German-Russians,
translated by Joseph S. Height
(Lincoln, Nebraska:
Reprint by the
American Historical
Society of
Germans from Russia, 1978).

was poor. Two of my sisters and one brother died during one winter. My father then built a new house out of small logs which we gathered from the hillsides on land adjoining our home place. We used a wooden plow to break the ground, made a packer of poles, and used brush we gathered to level the plowed ground. We seeded by hand, harvested the crops with a scythe, and tied the grain by hand. We hauled the crop into the barnyard and spread it on the ground and then pounded it with sticks. Then we would toss the chaff up in the wind so that the grain would sift down onto a blanket. This was slow work, but we managed to get along. The entire family helped out on these occasions. We cured our own meat and made all the soap we used out of tallow and pork cracklings.

When I was a young girl, I enjoyed dances and weddings in our neighborhood. I also remember fishing with nets at a lake close to our home. We would put in a supply of fish that would last us all winter. We also picked wild fruit in the summer months.

The Mennonite Experience in Cavalier County

The Spenst Family

Our family lived on barley bread and a beverage made from roasted barley.

The story of the Spenst family is representative of the Mennonite families who left Russia because the Tsar demanded that Germans serve in the Russian army. Jake Spenst was only ten in 1876 as Russia and Turkey headed toward war, but his father Jacob was certain that eventually his sons would have to go to war for Russia — and that would be contrary to his religious beliefs. Like many other German-Russian Mennonites, the Spensts farmed in Canada before homesteading in Cavalier County.

S O IN 1876, MOTHER AND FATHER AND SEVEN CHILDREN went by train to Hamburg, Germany, where we waited for ten days for other Russian emigrants. Among them was the Jacob Penner family.

From there, we continued to Liverpool, England where we were again delayed as we waited ten more days for other Russian peasants who were migrating to North America. Finally, we boarded a steamship bound for Quebec, Canada. We landed 21 days later. We traveled from Quebec by boat and train to Moorhead, Minnesota along with the Penner family and went on to Mapleton, Dakota Territory. From there, we went up the Red River to Rat Creek, Canada, where we were met by

John and Jake Abrahams and John Hamm. They took us to East Reserve, Canada.

Father filed on some land; and, with the aid of his neighbors, he built a 14- by 20-foot log house. The floors in this log house were made by partially embedding logs into the soil to form four equal boxes, which were filled with a sod-clay mixture to a height slightly above the top surface of the logs. The house was divided into two rooms by a hollow sod-brick wall into which father built a stove and oven which served more to heat the home than it did to divide the house. The stove-oven was three feet short of reaching the ceiling and six feet less than the width of the walls, which made possible a three-foot door at each side of the wall. Father made chairs and a table from crude lumber. One of the rooms was further divided into bedrooms by dividing the floor into equal squares with heavy logs. These squares were filled with hay which served as beds.

During the first several months in East Reserve, our family lived on barley bread and a beverage made from roasted barley. We could buy 600 pounds of barley-chop on credit from the Canadian government. Several months later, father bought a milch cow and a team of oxen. The next spring, melting snow forced us to abandon our claim. We hitched our oxen to a large, two-wheeled cart and hauled our belongings to higher ground.

Here, father built a 14- by 28-foot sod house with a gable roof. First, he dug a hole two and one-half feet deep. Then, he built walls six feet above the ground and extended the gables of sod bricks beyond the walls. He covered the roof of logs with long grass and sod bricks. He left an opening in each end wall for windows, the width of one brick (three feet) by about four feet, and space for a door three feet by six feet on one side.

The spring we arrived, father broke about eight acres of land and seeded it to wheat, flax, and barley. We harvested with a scythe, gathered the crop by hand, and threshed the grain with a flail, a homemade tool that was six feet long and slightly bigger than a hay fork. Attached to the handle was a three-foot long club. We cleaned the grain in the wind.

After two and one-half years in East Reserve, father was unable to pay the government loan, so he gave up his land to Cornelius Foth, who paid the debt. In March 1879, we moved to West Reserve, Manitoba, three miles northeast of Gretna, Manitoba. Here, father filed on a half-section of land. Until spring, we lived with father's brother, George. Then we built a sod house similar to the one in East Reserve. During that spring, I and my brothers broke 20 acres of land and seeded it into wheat, barley, and flax. We used my uncle's machinery.

In June 1879, I hired out to help Frank Keiwer, a schoolteacher, build a sod house and earned 15 cents a day.

During the next five years, father made enough money farming to build a house and barn of lumber and to buy a reaper, a binder, a plow, horses, a threshing machine and steam engine, and furnishings for the home.

I and my brothers reached manhood, and we wanted to acquire farms of our own. But the area we lived in no longer afforded opportunity to homestead, so we looked to Dakota Territory. Father, realizing that Dakota might give his boys a start in life, went south to investigate.

In October 1886, my father, a neighbor, Dave Veer, and I drove with horses and buggy to Cavalier County in Dakota Territory. We took food for the trip and saw many deer en route. Reaching a point west of Langdon, we decided to stake our claims. We made the round trip of 175 miles in four days.

The next summer in July, father, my brother, Uncle George, and I drove with horses to Cavalier County to stake our claims. We did not have to establish a home upon reaching the new land because Dave and John Veer, who had settled there in March, gave us accommodations.

Father filed on the west half of Section 21 — the SW¼ was his homestead, the NW¼ his tree claim. I claimed as my homestead the SE¼ of Section 21 and took as my tree claim the SE¼ of Section 22. George took the NE¼ of Section 21 as his homestead. At the junction of the four quarters in Section 21, George and I built a six- by 7-foot sod hovel. It was just large enough for two men to sleep in, and we used it only for this purpose, because the law required that a pioneer had to sleep on his land one night before he could file on his claim.

We made hay during the summer with machinery borrowed from Dave and John Veer. We also helped dig a well on Dave's homestead, work done with a spade and hand auger. When we got down 30 feet, the well filled with natural gas, so we had to alternate with each other every ten minutes in our digging so we wouldn't be asphyxiated. We reached water at 50 feet, where the gas disappeared.

That fall, we returned to Canada to help harvest the family crop. While we were there, we received, by mail at Gretna, notice that our claim at Langdon could be filed. We interrupted threshing in Canada for four days to file our claim in Dakota in September 1887.

In October, father, my four brothers, and I drove to Cavalier County to begin building a house and barn of lumber we bought in Neche for about $30 per thousand. It was hauled to our homestead by the Neche Transfer Company for $25 per 500-board-foot. We built a house 22- by 30-feet with a 10- by 22-foot lean shed at one end, which served as a kitchen. We furnished the home with a coal range, coal heater, table, chairs, beds, and cooking utensils we brought from our farm in Manitoba. The barn, 26- by 45-feet, was not completed that fall, but we did make what we finished weather-proof to shelter the horses.

The next spring, I broke 20 acres and seeded it to flax. We also dug a well 60 feet deep on father's place with a spade and hand-auger. During the summer of 1888, I built a 14- by 28-foot house on my homestead. Early frost damaged 90 percent of our flax crop, which sold in Langdon for 90 cents a bushel.

In 1889, I seeded wheat. The gophers were very numerous that year, and they damaged much of my crop. But a Fourth of July torrential downpour gave my grain new life. The heads filled out, and my crop produced 32 bushels per acre, in spite of being damaged by frost, as was my crop the following year.

In June 1891, I visited friends near Plum Coulee, Manitoba, where I met Margarite Penner for the first time since we came together from Russia. After several hours of renewing our acquaintance, we decided to marry. We went first to my homestead where Margarite saw for herself that she would have a future home and then to Mapleton, North Dakota, to the home of her parents, where we were wed on July 2. Accompanied by her sister Anna, we walked several miles to a wood to pick Juneberries. Despite my effort to keep close to my bride, I lost her in the thick foliage. Only after several hours of frantic searching and calling did I finally find her at the farm. On the Fourth of July, my bride and I returned by train to our homestead. En route, the conductor ordered the train stopped near Park River so I might have a dance with my bride. The engine of the train was decorated with tree branches to celebrate our marriage.

On April 15, 1892, our first child, Anna, was born. Our other children were Mary, June 10, 1893; and Margarite, May 7, 1895.

In 1894, I had a very good crop of wheat, 25 to 52 bushels per acre, which I sold in Langdon for 40 cents per bushel.

On December 31, 1896, my wife passed away. My oldest sister, Annie, took over responsibilities in my home until March 1897, when I hired Annie Bartell, who had just moved to our township from Hillsboro, Kansas, with her

German-Russian Mennonites and Their Horseless Buggy
Demonstrating their "flair for fun," two young men put syrup buckets on the front of a wagon, and took off the tongue — one holds what could be an old tractor steering wheel.
Photograph from **Plains Folk: North Dakota's Ethnic History**
(Fargo, North Dakota: North Dakota Institute for Regional Studies, 1988).

parents, Mr. and Mrs. John Bartell. On August 7th, Annie Bartell and I were married by her father, John Bartell, who was now the resident Mennonite minister in the township. We had fifteen children: Anna, April 12, 1898; Eva, August 6, 1900; Jake, Jr., May 10, 1902; John, July 5, 1904; Nora, March 9, 1906; Ella, November 17, 1907; Reuben, July 8, 1909; Edwin, January 11, 1913; Alma, March 10, 1916; Adeline, April 8,

Mennonite German-Russian School in Cavalier County, Circa 1912
Photograph from **Plains Folk: North Dakota's Ethnic History** *(Fargo, North Dakota: North Dakota Institute for Regional Studies, 1988).*

1918; Roland, June 1, 1920; Leona, February 11, 1922; Elroy, December 8, 1923; Jackqualine, March 10, 1925; and Vivian, January 18, 1928.

In 1900, I organized a "Farmers' Baseball Team." Prior to this, many of the pioneers in the vicinity had not seen a baseball game. Although I had seen several games in Langdon, I understood very little about baseball. Nonetheless, my team played all the towns in Cavalier County. About 1910, we had a really good team, and I hired a special train to take the club to Grand Forks to play the Grand Forks Nine.

I made a great deal of money farming in Cavalier County for 20 years. I built a larger home and a grain elevator to store my grain. Always interested in seeing idle land put under cultivation, I made many trips to Winnipeg, Manitoba, to urge immigration. Often, I would bring men back with me to look at the land in North Dakota.

In 1914, I invented a grain cleaner that separated barley from wheat, something that no other cleaner could do. I spent many years and thousands of dollars trying to get a patent. In 1917, I sold my farm and moved my family to Langdon, but I returned to living on the land once again.

From Selz to Selz and Trouble with Creditors

Balzar Thomas

ᗡ had no money,
so ᗡ looked for work at once.

Born in Selz in southern Russia on November 18, 1862, Balzar Thomas spent his boyhood working on his parents' farm. When he was 21, he served for a year in the Russian army. In 1885 he and his boyhood friend, Joseph Weisbeck, decided to leave for the United States. Weisbeck paid for the trip. After purchasing their tickets, they had three cents left and had to depend on fellow immigrants for food. Weisbeck and Thomas, as well as the nine families and five single men who accompanied them, left Russia because of the Tsar's policy of forced military training. Like many Black Sea Germans, they rebelled against unjust treatment.

OSEPH WEISBECK AND I along with several others arrived at New York harbor October 9, 1885. After passing inspection we proceeded to Ipswich, Dakota Territory, arriving on October 12, 1885. There were nine families and five single fellows in our party when we arrived at Ipswich.

I had no money, so I looked for work at once and found it with Adam Jungle, who had come to Dakota Territory in 1884 from the same village in Russia. He employed me for one year, paying me $110. I agreed to break ten acres for flax and seed it. The yield that year was fair, and I received in addition to my wages 100 bushes of flax, which I sold for $1.10 per bushel.

The threshing was done by horse power, and the separator was fed by hand. There was no blower on the separator, so the straw was moved away from the rear by two horses directed by a man behind a heavy square log which was dragged along the ground. The straw was dragged to the left and then to the right.

In 1887 I homesteaded in McIntosh County and built a sod house which I used for one year. Then I built a better home, knowing that my parents would soon join me. They arrived in 1888, and in 1889 I went into partnership with my father and mother in farming. We purchased another breaking plow and paid $42 for four ponies. That year we put in ten acres of wheat and ten acres of oats. We also broke fifty acres for flax to be seeded the next spring. The wheat and oats yielded well.

On June 24, 1890, I married Clara Uhrich, a daughter of Egethe Uhrich, neighbors to the west of me. The Uhrich family came from Alsace in 1886 and filed on some land.

Father Bernard Strassmeir, a resident priest of Fort Yates who also served our territory, officiated at the ceremony which took place in the McIntosh church.

By that time my father had found land for himself in Campbell County, Dakota Territory. My wife and I continued farming until 1895, when we quit. Turning my property over to my creditors, we left for Portland, Oregon. We returned from Portland in 1896 to Haegle Township, Pierce County, about 12 miles northeast of Harvey, around Selz.

On this new site we built a 12- by 14-foot shack out of lumber we hauled from Harvey. I faced the outside with homemade clay bricks and purchased three horses, a wagon, a cow, and a calf. I broke some land, but it was too late to seed that spring. I rented a mower and rake and put up some hay that summer, and that fall I worked out harvesting and threshing. After threshing I hitched two horses to the wagon and traveled about 30 miles to Pony Gulch and got a small load of very poor lignite coal. That winter we sat before the cookstove and twisted hay into hard knots and pushed it into the stove because the coal was so poor a grade that it would not burn alone.

In 1897 I seeded my first crop in Pierce County. The yield was fair, and the next year I seeded more. Luck seemed to be with me for a while. On leaving McIntosh territory I had taken it for granted that my former creditors were satisfied with the property I left them, but such was not the case. After they found out that I was located in North Dakota again and that I was forging ahead, they started action in court to collect additional money. I was served with papers; but, as this was an altogether new procedure for me, I did not appear in court. The creditors received a judgement against me for about $8,800. In due time I paid this because I did not want them to get possession of my new home.

Butchering on the Farm in Emmons County
Photographs above and below from **A History of Emmons County**
Compiled for the Bicentennial, 1976 by the Emmons County Historical Society.

A Second Boom Homesteader

Morris Weisgarber

The furniture was made out of boxes.

When he was two years old, Morris Weisgarber came to
America in 1889 with his parents, August and Madeline, who farmed near
Lundaf, Russia. Morris worked for his parents and other area farmers until he was 21 (1909). He then decided to homestead for himself as
newly-arrived immigrants began to swell the population of western North
Dakota. In 1910 he met and married Nellie Winchel who had emigrated
from Russia with her parents in 1900. Their homestead was not far from
Morris' place. As a young girl, Nellie worked on neighboring farms earning
enough money to buy her own clothes. Nellie and Morris raised eight children on the homestead.

MY FAMILY ARRIVED IN NORTH DAKOTA in the fall of 1889
and remained in Bismarck until the following spring. Our
winter quarters were quite simple — a two-room log house which was a
wreck that had not been used for many years. After spending two or
three weeks in repairing this building and making it quite comfortable,
we moved in. The furniture was made out of boxes, as my parents had
very little money left after the long, expensive trip from Russia. Father
managed to get steady employment during the winter, which provided
us with a living and about $100 in savings. The following spring father
selected his homestead and moved the family to this land where he built

88

Morris Weisgarber with Horses in Front of Rock & Clay Barn
From **Oliver County: 1885-1985**, *a publication of the*
Oliver County Historical Society, 1985.

a small shack out of lumber by exchanging work with some of his neighbors. He managed to break some 20 acres the first year, which he seeded to flax and wheat. He bought a few cows and some chickens. In a few years, the home place built up in good shape.

In the winter of 1896, father and I had a terrible experience on a trip to Bismarck. We left home in the morning with the team and sleigh. it was nice, clear weather, but when we were on our way back home that afternoon over snow that was three- or four-feet deep, a blizzard came up with a strong wind from the northwest. We could not face the storm and lost our bearings on road. We wandered over the prairie for several hours. When our horses became exhausted, we unhitched them and turned them loose. As we had plenty of robes along, we upset the wagon box and crawled underneath and covered ourselves. There we stayed until the following afternoon when the storm finally quieted down. We found our horses a half-mile away, dead and buried in the snow up to their ears. We walked over to a farm a quarter-mile away. The farmer took his team and sleigh and helped us shovel out our horses. We removed the harness and picked up the supples we had bought in town. We finally got home that night. Some time later we went back and brought home our own sleigh and returned the team and sleigh we borrowed.

After I saved about $400, I decided, in 1909, to get a home of my own. I filed on a homestead north of Mandan in Oliver County, close to the Yucca Post Office. I married Nellie Winchel, who was also a German from Russia, the following spring. We moved onto our homestead with a team of horses, some old machinery, and the household goods I had accumulated and built a small house. Later, I built a barn out of sod and clay-mud. I broke about 12 acres the first year and seeded it to flax. It produced 14 bushels to the acre. I also bought two cows; they furnished plenty of milk and butter for our living. We got lots of eggs from 25 chickens.

I had several good crops the first 15 years and made a good living in Oliver County. I improved the farm buildings, bought adjoining land, and purchased new machinery.

Oxen Were Seldom Seen in Towns During the Second Boom
From the Fred Hultstrand History in Pictures Collection, NDIRS-NDSU, Fargo, N.D.

Index of Places, Origins, Conditions, and Travel

PLACES (North Dakota or Dakota Territory unless otherwise noted)

Counties
Campbell, 86
Cavalier, 79, 81, 84
Dickey, 27, 30, 36
Emmons, 1, 4, 5-6, 8, 14, 25, 41, 87
Faulk, 8
Foster, 60
Logan, 23- 24
McHenry, 62
McIntosh, 21, 36, 64, 70, 71, 86
Oliver, 74, 76, 90
Pierce, 41, 46-47, 86, 87
Tripp (SD), 26
Wells, 53-56, 60, 62-63

Townships
Antelope, 36, 65
Antelope Valley, 21
Fairville, 60
Germantown, 60
Haegle, 86
Odessa, 8
Oshkosh, 63
Springfield, 71
Whitestone, 30
Woodward, 60

Towns
Anamoose, 62
Baltimore, MD, 34
Bismarck, 10
Capel, Manitoba, 60
Carrington, 53-55, 59-61

More Towns . . .
Cathay, 54-55
Chicago, 28, 34
Columbus, SD, 56
Duluth, MN, 50
East Reserve, Manitoba, 80
Edgeley, 24-25, 30
Ellendale, 21, 31, 36-37, 39, 65-67,71, 73
Eureka, 1, 3, 13, 15-16, 28
Fessenden, 63
Fort Yates, 86
Grand Forks, 84
Gretna, Manitoba, 81-82
Hague, 45, 47
Harvey, 86
Hazelton, 4
Hoskins, 36, 71
Ipswich, 85
Keystone, 31
Kulm, 20-22, 31, 40, 73
Langdon, 82-84
Lesterfield, 29
Lincoln, NE, 56
Linton, 9, 10
Lodi, CA, 51
Mandan, 75-76, 90
Mapleton, 79, 82
Max, 22
Medicine Hat, Saskatchewan, 51

More Towns . . .
Melville, 62
Moffit, 4
Monango, 21, 31-32
Moorhead, MN, 79
New York City, 13, 19, 24, 27-28, 50, 59, 65, 70, 75
Parkston, 30, 35-36, 70
Plum Coulee, Manitoba, 82
Portland, OR, 86
Quebec, Canada, 79
Rat Creek, Manitoba, 79
Scotland, 28-29, 34, 70
Selz, 86
Strasburg, 2
Sykeston, 53-54
Temvik, 4-5
Tindle, 29
Tripp, 29
Velva, 22
Wayside, WI, 19
West Reserve, Manitoba, 81
Westfield, 4
Williamsport, 9-10, 14
Willow City, 50
Winnipeg, Manitoba, 60, 84
Yankton, 8
Yucca Post Office, 89

Russian Origin of Settlers
Blumenthal (Volhynia), 48
Berrsena, 64
Denovitz, 23
Dobrudja, 58
Gnadenfelt, 33
Katerena, 77
Kiev, 52
Kulm, 11, 33, 69
Lundaf, 88
Mansburg, 19
Monheim, 41-42
Odessa, 75
Selz, 7, 85
Strassburg, 1, 3

Conditions in Russia
8, 11, 23, 49, 59, 64, 75, 77

Conditions in Turkey-Rumania
59

Travel from Russia
12-13, 24, 27, 33-34, 42-43, 50, 53, 65-66, 69-70, 75, 79

Travel to Dakota by Train
8, 13, 27-28, 34, 43-44, 50, 70

Travel in Dakota
8, 30, 36, 65-67, 70-71

Index of Churches, Schools, Land Claiming, Farming, Homestead Houses & Households, Disaster and Weather, Death & Seasickness, Trouble with Creditors, and Recreation

Churches/Religion

Eureka Evangelical Church,
  help from, 17
German Baptist Church,
  building of, 60-61
Greek Catholic, 50
McIntosh Church, wedding, 86
Mennonite, 83
Seventh Day Adventist education, 56
Springfield Township, first services, 72

Schools

Mennonite School, 84
Poor children
  tormented, 17
Russian, 49
Turkish, 62
Woodward School
  District, 56

Land Claiming

14, 31-32, 46-47, 62, 81

Farming & Gathering

Breaking Sod
21, 26, 32, 36-37, 50, 63, 76, 80-81, 86, 89
Harvesting
15, 32, 37, 39, 51, 55, 62, 67, 76,
  78, 80, 82-83
Hired Hand Work
16, 22, 67
Picking Buffalo Bones
25, 37, 65-67, 72-73
Picking Juneberries
83
Raising Chickens
67-68, 89

**Homestead Houses
& Households**

1, 4, 14-15, 21, 24-26, 31, 34-36,
  39-40, 50, 53, 60, 65, 68, 71-72,
  75, 80-82, 86, 90

Food Preparation

15, 17, 19, 21, 38,
  71, 75, 80

Making Clothing

25, 54, 77

Disaster and Weather

Blizzards
1, 29, 37-39, 55, 89
Drought
15, 17
General Comments on
25, 29, 35, 45, 82
Mosquitoes
71
Prairie Fires
4-5, 25

Death

Flegel son, August,
  killed by lightning, 18
Johnson and son burned to death, 6
Klebe daughter, 51
Kraft infant, 12
Mosbrucker relatives, 78
Margarite Spenst, 83

Seasickness

13, 24, 43, 65

Trouble with Creditors

17, 21, 32, 87

Recreation

Baseball, 84
Dancing, 78
Reading, 29
Visiting, 35

About the editors . . .

Historian D. Jerome Tweton returned to his hometown, Grand Forks, North Dakota, to teach in the University of North Dakota history department in 1965 after receiving his Ph.D. from the University of Oklahoma. For most of his thirty-year tenure at the University, he served as department chairman. Tweton's books include The Marquis de Morès: Dakota Capitalist, French Nationalist *and* The New Deal at the Grassroots: Programs for the People in Otter Tail County, Minnesota. *A senior consultant to the North Dakota state partner of the National Endowment for the Humanities, Tweton has written and edited books and articles about the history of North Dakota for citizens of all ages, including text books and instructional material for classroom use. In addition to his work as an academic historian who has edited publications, written seven books and scores of articles, Tweton has participated in over 300 public humanities programs in North Dakota and throughout the nation. He and his wife Paula own and operate a bed-and-breakfast in a renovated turn-of-the-century home which is on the National Register of Historic Places, the Beiseker Mansion in Fessenden, North Dakota.*

Everett C. Albers has served as the executive director of The North Dakota Humanities Council, the state partner of the National Endowment for the Humanities, since it began in 1973. Albers is one of the founders of the modern Chautauqua movement which features first-person characterizations of historical writers and thinkers presented in tents during summer tours of the Great Plains. He holds an M.A. in English from Colorado State University and has taught humanities and English. A North Dakota native who grew up on a family homestead in Oliver County, Albers lives with his wife Leslie in Bismarck. They are the parents of Albert and Gretchen. Albers operates Otto Design, a desktop publishing concern, and the publishing house Northern Lights, ND Press, as an avocation. He co-edited The Legacy of North Dakota Country Schools *and the 1998* Behold Our New Century: Early 20th Century Visions of America *and has written several children's coloring books featuring Seaman, the dog who went with Lewis and Clark, as well as the 2002* The Saga of Seaman: The Story of the Dog Who Went with Lewis & Clark.